THE MASONIC BOOK CLUB

— VOL. 5 —

A Serious and Impartial Enquiry into the Cause of the Present Decay of Free-Masonry in the Kingdom of Ireland

Fifield D'Assigny

Westphalia Press
An Imprint of the Policy Studies Organization
Washington, DC

A Serious and Impartial Enquiry into the Cause of the Present Decay of Free-Masonry in the Kingdom of Ireland

All Rights Reserved © 2025 by Policy Studies Organization

Westphalia Press
An imprint of Policy Studies Organization
1367 Connecticut Avenue NW
Washington, D.C. 20036
info@ipsonet.org

ISBN: 978-1-63723-578-2

Daniel Gutierrez-Sandoval, Executive Director
PSO and Westphalia Press

Updated material and comments on this edition can be found at the Westphalia Press website:
www.westphaliapress.org

The Masonic Book Club

The *Masonic Book Club* (MBC) was formed in 1970 by two Illinois Masons, Alphonse Cerza, 33°, and Louis L. Williams, 33°. The MBC primarily reprinted out-of-print Masonic books with scholarly introductions; occasionally they would print additional texts as "bonuses" (though none were marked specifically as such on the title pages); sometimes a reprint would be marked "Masonic Book Club Edition"; often an unnumbered bonus was published jointly with the Illinois Lodge of Research or the Supreme Council, 33°, NMJ, USA.

Most of the MBC volumes indicated on the title page, "Volume [*Number*] of the Publications of the Masonic Book Club," some were misnumbered, and some were unnumbered. Indeed, the numbering of the early volumes was inconsistent. For example, *A Serious and Impartial Enquiry* is "Volume Five" (1974) but *Masonic Membership of the Founding Fathers* is "The Masonic Book Club Edition" (1974). Then, *Masonry Dissected* is "Volume Eight" (1977), *The Trestleboard* is "Volume 8A" (1978), and *Anderson's Constitutions of 1738* is "Volume Nine" (1978). If nothing else, MBC books keep bibliophiles on their toes.

The first volumes had deckle-edged paper and pages of slightly different sizes, though eventually the MBC settled into a 6″×9″ trimmed-page format for their books. The books were bound in a dark blue fabric with gold lettering. Listed below are the fifty-nine MBC volumes published 1970–2010 with bonuses. N.B.: A number and letter, e.g. "Volume 8A," is a numbering for this reprint series.

The club originally was limited to 333 members, but the number grew to nearly 2,000, with 1,083 members when it dissolved in 2010. In 2017 MW Barry Weer, 33°, the last president of the MBC, transferred the MBC name and assets to the Supreme Council, 33°, SJ, USA. Under the editorship of Arturo de Hoyos, 33°, G∴C∴, and S. Brent Morris, 33°, G∴C∴, the revived Masonic Book Club has the goal of publishing classic Masonic books while supporting Scottish Rite, SJ, USA philanthropies.

Publications of the Masonic Book Club, 1970–2010

1	1970	*The Regius Poem*	Masonic Book Club
2	1971	*The Constitutions of the Free-Masons*	Benjamin Franklin
3	1972	*Ahiman Rezon*	Laurence Dermott
4	1973	*Illustrations of Masonry*	William Preston
5	1974	*A Serious and Impartial Enquiry into the Cause of the Present Decay of Free-Masonry in the Kingdom of Ireland*	Fifield D'Assigny
5A	1974*	*Masonic Membership of the Founding Fathers*	Ronald E. Heaton

6	1975	*The Signers of the Declaration of Independence*	David C. Whitney
7	1976	*The Signers of the Constitution of the United States*	David C. Whitney
7A	1976*	*Masonic Symbols in American Decorative Art*	Louis L. Williams & Alphonse Cerza
8	1977	*Samuel Prichard's Masonry Dissected, 1730*	Harry Carr
8A	1978*	*Trestle-Board (A facsimile of the original Trestle Board by the Baltimore Masonic Convention of 1843)*	Dwight L. Smith
9	1978	*Anderson's Constitutions of 1738*	Lewis Edward & W. J. Hughan
10	1979	*Sufferings of John Coustos*	Wallace McLeod
11	1980	*The Revelations of a Square*	George Oliver
11A	1980	*Biblical Characters in Freemasonry*	John H. Van Gorden
11B	1980*	*A Masonic Reader's Guide*	*Guide* Alphonse Cerza & Thomas Warden
12	1981	*Three Distinct Knocks and Jachin and Boaz*	Harry Carr
13	1982	*Masonic Almanacs and Anti-Masonic Almanacs*	Plez A. Transou
13A	1982*	*Stephen A. Douglas: Freemason*	Wayne C. Temple
14	1983	*The Beginnings of Freemasonry in America*	Melvin M. Johnson
14A	1983*	*Bespangled, Painted & Embroidered: Decorated Masonic Aprons in America, 1790–1850*	Scottish Rite Masonic Museum & Library
14B	1983*	*Making a Mason at Sight*	Louis L. Williams
15	1984	*Masonic Concordance of the Holy Bible*	Charles Clyde Hunt
15A	1984*	*By Square and Compasses: The Building of Lincoln's Home and Its Saga*	Wayne C. Temple

16	1985	*The Old Gothic Constitutions*	Wallace McLeod
16A	1985*	*Modern Historical Characters in Freemasonry*	John H. Van Gorden
17	1986	*The Rise and Development of Organised Freemasonry*	Roy A. Wells
17A	1986*	*Ancient and Early Medieval Historical Characters in Freemasonry*	John H. Van Gorden
18	1987	*The Lodge in Friendship Village and Other Stories*	P. W. George
18A	1987*	*Masonic Charities*	John H. Van Gorden & Stewart M. L. Pollard
18B	1987*	*Medieval Historical Characters in Freemasonry*	John H. Van Gorden
18C	1987*	*George Washington in New York*	Allan Boudreau & Alexander Bleimann
19	1988	*Records of the Hole Crafte and Fellowship of Masons*	Edward Conder, Jr.
20	1989	*A Candid Disquisition of the Principles and Practices of the Most Ancient and Honourable Society of Free and Accepted Masons*	Wellins Calcott
20A	1989*	*Freemasonry and Nauvoo, 1839–1846*	Robin L. Carr
21	1990	*Masonic Odes and Poems*	Rob Morris
22	1991	*Lessing's Masonic Dialogues*	Gotthold Lessing
22A	1991*	*ABC of Freemasonry: A Book for Beginners*	Delmar D. Darrah
23	1992	*The Folger Manuscript*	S. Brent Morris
24	1993	*Freemasonry and Christianity: Lectures from Two Ages*	T. De Witt Peake & John J. Murchison
25	1994	*The Constitutions of St. John's Lodge*	Robin L. Carr
25A	1994*	*The Mystic Tie and Men of Letters*	Robin L. Carr
26	1995	*Recollections of a Masonic Veteran*	S. Brent Morris

27	1996	*The Freemason's Monitor or Illustrations of Masonry in Two Parts*	Thomas Smith Webb
28	1997	*The Masonic Ladder or the Nine Steps to Ancient Freemasonry*	John Sherer
28A	1997*	*Freemasonry and Democracy: Its Evolution in North America*	Allen E. Roberts & Wallace McLeod
29	1998	*The Masonic Harp: Collection of Masonic Odes, Hymns, Songs*	George Wingate Chase
30	1999	*Symbolic Teachings of Masonry and Its Message*	Thomas Milton Stewart
31	2000	*Freemasonry Its Meaning and Significance, An Exposition of its Ethics, Religion and Philosophy*	Otto Caspari
32	2001	*K. R. Cama Masonic Jubilee Volume*	Jivanji Jamshedji Modi
33	2002	*Caementaria Hibernica*	W. J. Chetwode Crawley
34	2003	*A Daily Advancement in Masonic Knowledge*	Wallace McLeod & S. Brent Morris
35	2004	*The Craftsman, and Templar's Textbook and, also, Melodies for the Craft*	Cornelius Moore
36	2005	*The Text Book of Freemasonry*	Retired Member of the Craft
37	2006	*Orations of the Illustrious Brother Frederick Dalcho Esq., M.D.*	Frederick Dalcho
38	2007	*Antiquities of Freemasonry Comprising Illustrations of the Five Grand Periods of Masonry from the Creation of the World to the Dedication of King Solomon's Temple*	George Oliver
39	2008	*Diogenes' Lamp or an Examination of our Present-Day Morality and Enlightenment*	Adam Weishaupt
40	2009	*Proofs of Conspiracy Against All the Governments of Europe*	John Robison
41	2010	*The Evolution of Freemasonry*	Delmar Darrah

* indicates a bonus book

A Serious and Impartial Enquiry into the
Cause of the Present Decay of Free-Masonry
in the Kingdom of Ireland

D'Assigny

[This text appeared in the original edition.]

This volume has been published
solely for the Members of
The Masonic Book Club
and is limited to
888 copies
of which this is
No._____

© 1974, by The Masonic Book Club
Printed in the United States of America

A Serious and Impartial Enquiry into the
Cause of the Present Decay of Free-Masonry
in the Kingdom of Ireland, 1744

An Answer to the Pope's Bull; with the
Character of a Free-Mason, 1738

An Impartial Answer to the Enemies of
Free-Masonry, 1741

by Fifield D'Assigny

together with

The General Regulations of the Free and
Accepted Masons in the Kingdom of Ireland, 1744

and

A Pocket Companion for Free-Masons, 1735

VOLUME FIVE
of the publications of
THE MASONIC BOOK CLUB

Published by
THE MASONIC BOOK CLUB
A Not-for-Profit Corporation of Illinois
Bloomington, Illinois
1974

Table of Contents

LIST OF ILLUSTRATIONS.................................... vii

ACKNOWLEDGMENTS....................................... ix

PREFACE.. xi

A COMMENTARY—J. FAIRBAIRN SMITH....................... 1

A SERIOUS AND IMPARTIAL ENQUIRY, ETC. 19

INTRODUCTION AND COMMENTARY TO *An Answer to the Pope's Bull, 1738* and *An Impartial Answer to the Enemies of Freemasonry, 1741*—R. E. PARKINSON........................ 49

ANSWER TO THE POPE'S BULL, 1738........................ 65

AN IMPARTIAL ANSWER TO THE ENEMIES OF FREE-MASONRY, 1741... 71

THE GENERAL REGULATIONS, ETC. 87

A POCKET COMPANION FOR FREE-MASONS.................... 123

OFFICERS OF THE MASONIC BOOK CLUB...................... 161

ROSTER OF MEMBERS OF THE MASONIC BOOK CLUB........... 163

COLOPHON.. 173

List of Illustrations

THE ILLUSTRATIONS LISTED BELOW ARE FACSIMILE REPRODUCTIONS
OF THE ORIGINAL PRINTINGS OF THESE PAGES

TITLE PAGE TO *A Serious and Impartial Enquiry*............ 19
TITLE PAGE TO *An Answer to the Pope's Bull*.............. 64
FRONTISPIECE TO *An Impartial Answer*..................... 70
TITLE PAGE TO *An Impartial Answer*....................... 71
TITLE PAGE TO *The General Regulations*................... 87
FRONTISPIECE TO *A Pocket Companion*..................... 122
TITLE PAGE TO *A Pocket Companion*....................... 123

Acknowledgments

The Masonic Book Club and its Editors are deeply grateful to Ill.˙.J. Fairbairn Smith, 33°, F.P.S., for his permission to reproduce his rare copy of *A Serious and Impartial Enquiry, etc., The General Regulations, etc.,* and *A Pocket Companion, etc.* together with his learned Commentary thereon; and to

Quatuor Coronati Lodge No. 2076 of London, and its Master and Editor, Brother Roy A. Wells, for permission to use the article by Brother R. E. Parkinson and the D'Assigny pamphlets reproduced in Volume 77 of *Ars Quatuor Coronatum*. Without their gracious help and cooperation, this volume would have been impossible.

Preface

This fifth volume of the Masonic Book Club presents material that is rare and not easily accessible to the average Masonic reader. Dr. D'Assigny's works are not earth-shattering. His literary effort should be read in the light of the days in which he lived. They caused only a faint ripple in a narrow field when they were published, and very promptly dropped from sight, only to be unearthed over a century later. They are curiosities, yet; but most interesting curiosities. His *Serious and Impartial Enquiry* engages in the usual flights of historical fantasy, after the pattern so well initiated by Dr. James Anderson a few years before. His *Answer to the Pope's Bull* and his *Answer to the Enemies of Free-Masonry* may have required more courage than most of us realize today. So let us not underestimate the effect such a strong defense of the Craft might have had upon the readers of that day.

As we prepared to issue this, our fifth book, your editors were faced with an important decision. All four of our first books were facsimile reprints, reproducing the quaint typography of the eighteenth century. The English language is in a fluid state always, and the difference in phraseology is striking enough, while the difficulty of reading books two hundred years old is greatly increased by the use of the letter "s", which was printed as a so-called long "s", reading exactly like an "f", and rather confusing. So rather than reproduce D'Assigny in the old style, and in facsimile, we decided for the sake of convenience in reading, to set his broadside in modern letterpress, preserving the flavor by reproducing the title-pages. We have, however, retained the old style spelling, where used, and this should enhance the flavor of the olden style of writing. We trust that you, our members, will approve, and that you will enjoy this flavor of Fifield D'Assigny as he expounded to his Brother Masons, their friends and their enemies, his opinions and his feelings and his love for the "gentle craft".

Brother James Fairbairn Smith, who wrote a wonderful analysis for our first volume, *The Regius Poem*, has again demonstrated his outstanding ability as a historian and scholar by supplying the comment on D'Assigny. It is at his suggestion that we have adopted the spelling of our author's name as "D'Assigny" rather than "Dassigny". Brother Smith, doughty Scotsman that he is, has shown his Hibernian affinity in his sympathetic treatment of our Irish Doctor, Fifield D'Assigny, God rest him.

In 1964, Quatuor Coronati Lodge No 2076, in its volume 77, printed facsimile reproductions of D'Assigny's *An Answer to the Pope's Bull*, and *An Impartial Answer to the Enemies of Free-Masonry*, with a fine critical study of these pamphlets by Brother R. E. Parkinson. His dissertations on these two works by D'Assigny leave little room for comment, for his research has been painstaking and thorough. We are deeply indebted to Brother Roy A. Wells, Master and present Editor, and to Quatuor Coronati Lodge No. 2076 for permission to reproduce the text and Brother Parkinson's article thereon.

It seemed appropriate to your editors, after spending so much time with the Irish, to add the two items, *The General Regulations* and *A Pocket Companion*. This latter was written by one William Smith, an English Mason, about whom little else is known. Published in Dublin in 1735, it was the forerunner of a large group of such pocket-sized works published every few years thereafter. Containing as it does, a brief "History: Charges, Regulations, Song," etc., it was a cheap copy of Anderson's *Constitutions*, and caused that worthy brother to complain to his own Grand Lodge that Smith had committed the un-Masonic act of stealing his book. It marks another, if clandestine, landmark in the history of Masonic book publication.

Now, good reading and pleasant days.

Louis L. Williams
Alphonse Cerza

D'Assigny

A COMMENTARY

D'Assigny's Enquiry — Serious, Impartial

Stresses Decay, Warns, Protests, Suggests Reforms, Professes Esteem for Beauties of High Degrees

J. FAIRBAIRN SMITH, P.M., 33°, F.P.S.

> "*Ennobled by the name they bear,
> Distinguished by the badge they wear.*"

In spite of his oft professed disdain for the character of Fifield D'Assigny, Laurence Dermott, Irish Freemason who became the strong voice, arm, and guiding spirit of England's Antient Grand Lodge, nevertheless gives us the first intimation of the contents of Fifield D'Assigny's "Serious and Impartial Enquiry, etc." when in 1756 he (Dermott) compiled his "Ahiman Rezon" for the Antients, and to prove his point that the Royal Arch could not be properly conferred upon any candidate without his having passed the Chair in regular form according to the Ancient Custom of the Craft, Dermott actually proceeds to quote from the D'Assigny book as follows:

> Some of the Fraternity have expressed an uneasiness at this Matter being kept a Secret from them (since they had already passed through the usual Degrees of Probation). I cannot help being of Opinion that they have no Right to any such Benefit until they make a proper Application, and are received with due Formality: And as it is an organized Body of Men who have passed the Chair, and given undeniable Proofs of their skill in Architecture, it can-

not be treated with too much Reverence; and more especially since the Characters of the present Members of that particular Lodge are untainted, and their Behaviour judicious and unexceptionable: So that there cannot be the least Hinge to hang a Doubt on, but that they are most excellent Masons. (Enquiry, 13 lines bottom of page 23, two lines top of page 33.)

The above quotation embodied all that was known of D'Assigny and his works for considerably more than a century. The work itself had apparently completely disappeared, for a copy of it was not found until Brother William J. Hughan, who is now justly regarded as the father of English Masonic history, recognized and identified a copy of the long missing and greatly questioned "Enquiry" in 1874. For another quarter of a century it remained the only known original; however, in 1892 a second copy was discovered and a third in 1896.

Name Copy For Watson

Brother William Watson secured the copy of 1892 for the prestigious Masonic Library of West Yorkshire. With this copy was bound the only known complete set of the June 24, 1741 General Regulations of the Grand Lodge of Ireland. It is by far the most perfect of the three originals thus far found, for conjecture tells us that only the curious copperplate frontispiece suitable to the order and design seems to be missing.

It is from this unique source of rare book treasures of the Provincial Grand Lodge of West Yorkshire Masonic Library and by the courtesy of Brother William Watson that photographic reproduction was permitted and the 1893 Hughan-Jackson edition of the "Enquiry" plus the 1741 General Regulations of the Irish Grand Lodge were made available to an anxiously waiting Masonic public.

The Hughan-Jackson edition of the D'Assigny "Enquiry" has in turn become extremely scarce and the Masonic Book Club has been allowed the privilege of reproducing the "Enquiry" and General Regulations of Ireland from the Hughan-Jackson edition owned by Brother James Fairbairn Smith of Detroit. The reprint will also include a commentary on the Enquiry, which has up to this time been lacking.

It Warns, It Protests

As labeled, the "Enquiry" is indeed "Serious and Impartial," in that it calls for considerable reforms (some of which were made), it warns, it protests, it mourns decay, it philosophizes, it stresses the guidelines of the Craft, and emphatically calls attention to the tenets as specified by the Constitutions and General Regulations; it protests the appearance of imposters and attempts to exclude them from all deliberations. Moreover, in spite of adverse discussions in Grand Lodge circles, D'Assigny, in speaking of the multiple degree trend, gives his approbation and professes esteem for anyone who "shall add to the beauty of our glorious Art." We herewith quote his declaration concerning this phase of his "Enquiry" (page 33):

> I cannot help informing the Brethren that there is lately arrived in this city a certain itinerant Mason, whose judgment (as he declares) is so far illumin'd, and whose optics are so strong that they can bear the view of the most lucid rays of the sun at noon day, and altho' we have contented ourselves with three material steps to approach our Summum Bonum, the Immortal GOD, yet he presumes to acquaint us that he can add three more, which when properly plac'd may advance us to the highest heavens . . .

MISLED BY FALSE INSINUATIONS

> For my part I shall always profess a very great esteem for any one who shall add to the beauty of our glorious art, or by any means improve or enhance the value thereof, and were I assured that this adept had skill sufficient to demonstrate the truth of his assertion, I should pay him the utmost veneration; but until then he must excuse me from being one of his devotees, and I hope that no innocent and worthy Brother may at any time be misled by false insinuations, or foreign schemes.

At the top of page 32 we find that D'Assigny warns the Dublin Masons about an imposter who made a pretense of being a Master of the Royal Arch, which he asserted he brought with him from the city of York, but learned and wise discovered his fallacious art by a Mason from London who had:

> . . . some small space before attained that excellent part of Masonry in London and plainly proved that his doctrine was false . . . (and he was) . . . excluded from all benefits of the Craft. (Enquiry, page 32.)

Evidence at this time is available to show that in the early years of the 18th century Freemasonry was attracting some of the best and most stable elements in society. A society that boasts of the best will always have charms for the unworthy, and the brethren were soon faced with the necessity of adopting stern measures to ensure that only men of good character should be allowed entrance into Masonry. Dr. D'Assigny in 1744 voiced the idea of creating an Investigation or Inspection Committee by using these words:

SCABBY SHEEP MAY INFECT

I cannot help expressing my concern to hear of so many idle and trifling disputes as lately have happened amongst some of the Fraternity, occasioned, as I must imagine, by the unfortunate and inconsiderate election of their members; the examples of whom ought highly to engage us in a strict examination of the temper, disposition, and conduct of each candidate . . . as the old Proverb alledges, "One scabby sheep may infect an whole flock." (Enquiry, pages 28-29.)

Twenty-four years later D'Assigny's idea was finally adopted by the Grand Lodge of Ireland to be used in the metropolis of Dublin. It was added as Rule XIII of the Regulations of 1768.

Perhaps the need to correct candidate material by eliminating all unsuitable applicants may have occurred to D'Assigny as he looked in retrospect at his own background, for surely at that time an almost comatose conscience might have been moved to prick. The D'Assigny biography was far from being faultless.

Probably the real reason why D'Assigny in his "Enquiry" stressed the need for an investigation or inspection committee to ensure that only men of good character should be allowed access to Masonic membership was due to the happenings of the times, which to say the least could not be construed as being harmonious, when in 1740 dissension between contending powerful sources caused an ugly schism in Grand Lodge to rear its head.

Elect Lord, Viscount Doneraile

The records of the years 1740 to 1743 are told in two different versions. Both versions elect the Right Honorable Arthur Mohun,

Lord, Viscount Doneraile, as Grand Master of Ireland and both state the election was unanimous, but two meetings held on June 24, 1740, show that in spite of the pretended unanimity a dissident force led by the Right Honorable Richard, Earl of Anglesey, and the retiring Grand Master, Lord Viscount Mountjoy, and the so-called more aristocratic section of Grand Lodge, including "three late Grand Masters" might have caused grave problems.

An installation meeting of the regular Grand Lodge was called to meet at the regular place of assembly—the Grand Lodge room in Smith's Hall in Smock Alley, Dublin, and proceeded to induct Viscount Doneraile as Grand Master in due and ancient form. Doneraile in turn appointed his Deputy and Grand Wardens and officially declared them installed. Grand Lodge then decreed that "such lodges as have not already taken out Warrants were ordered to apply to John Baldwin, Secretary, to avoid the possibility of being proceded against as Rebel Masons."

Schism Develops

The dissident Anglesey group met on the same day, June 24, 1740, in Rose Tavern on Castle Street and the retiring Grand Master, Viscount Mountjoy, caused the name of Richard, Earl of Anglesey to be placed in nomination for Grand Master, declared him duly elected, and immediately installed him as the new Grand Master of Masons in Ireland and as a counterblast to the actions taken by the regular Grand Lodge decreed that: "all Free and Accepted Masons who are desirous of holding regular Lodges are ordered to apply to Mr. James Hewlet, Secretary, for proper Warrants, who is directed not to take any fee or reward."

Viscount Doneraile appears to have been the popular candidate for Grand Master and by 1743 the dispute had been completely settled to the satisfaction of all. Reading between the lines, it would seem obvious that D'Assigny as the writer of the "Serious and Impartial Enquiry" must have been moved to make an effort which would inspire the Craft to avoid such dissident acts in the future. In any event, by 1745 the veteran Mason John, 4th Lord Kingston, "like an affectionate and tender Brother, always ready to espouse the Cause of Truth, Charity, and Virtue" once more came forward and served as Grand Master.

Multiplicity of Degrees

As we close this phase of our Commentary on D'Assigny's "Serious and Impartial Enquiry," we note that it may have been composed with an eye to the elimination of such recent dissensions, but we feel that while his jeremiad deals with the unsuitability of candidates, at the same time it seems mainly to stress the pros and cons of the multiplicity of degrees, for on a previous page he (D'Assigny) took special care to remind his readers that a visiting Brother had pointed out that while Irish Masons have contented themselves with the "three material steps" it seems that the visitor was so knowledgeable that he could "add three more, which when properly placed may advance us to the highest heavens." (Enquiry, page 33.)

D'Assigny then goes on to add, "For my part I shall always profess a very great esteem for any one who shall add to the beauty of our glorious art, or by any means improve or enhance the value thereof." (Enquiry, page 33.)

As to the Decay of the Order, D'Assigny believed firstly it was due to poor investigation of candidates and suggested that one full month should elapse after election of applicants before degree work is conferred.

Secondly he was sure that the revival of the custom of visitation of lodges by the Grand Lodge officers would ensure the preservation of that "due harmony and just decorum which ought to shine amongst us."

A third cause for the "Decay" that was evident on every hand was the failure to properly observe the ancient landmarks of the Craft and enforce inspection of all books and the "Character and Conservations" of the members thereof.

The reader, if he should be alert, will note that D'Assigny did pen another Masonic literary work, the designation of which is mentioned on the title page of the "Enquiry" which specifically makes him the author. It is referred to as the "Impartial Answer to the Enemies of Free-Masons." This mention constitutes completely the sum total of our information about it until May, 1964, when the knowledgeable R. E. Parkinson, author of the second volume of the History of Freemasonry in Ireland, brings to the attention of the members of Quatuor Coronati Lodge No. 2076, the world's premier Lodge of Research, a paper which presents two rare Irish documents discovered in a volume of miscellaneous pamphlets in the Library of Queens University at Belfast. The discovery brought into focus a hitherto unknown, anonymous "Answer to the Pope's Bull of 1738" and the long lost "Impartial Answer to the Enemies of Freemasonry" by Dr. Fifield D'Assigny, published in 1741, both of which are definitely worth bringing to the attention of the Craft. The "Impartial Answer" was published by authority of the Grand Lodge of Ireland and read in Grand Lodge, April 1, 1741, and was a work of considerable merit.

Ecossais (Scots) Ceremonies

We purposely digress at this time to stress that the turmoil concerning the additional degrees has made its presence known in England and to a smaller extent in Scotland. Even the Royal Arch had a large number of enemies and without the rival Antient Grand Lodge of England and the appearance of the Irish Masonic expert Laurence Dermott, the Royal Arch would have had difficulty surviving. Hughan from the standpoint of the "Enquiry" has covered this phase of Masonic history amply and we now turn our attention to the insistent desires for sunlight and breathing space for the struggling Ecossais (Scots) ceremonies then extant in the British Isles.

From time to time historians have attempted to trace a native French Freemasonry back to mystical associations known as the Compagnonage; however, Masonic historians have long ago discarded such a theory as having not even the slightest probability.

From Same Legendary Store

In 1918 when J. E. Shum Tuckett was Senior Warden of Quatuor Coronati Lodge of Research he made the following three statements in his work entitled "The Origin of Additional Degrees" beginning on page 5 of Volume XXXII of A.Q.C.:

> 1. That before 1717 Freemasonry possessed a store of legend, tradition and symbolism of wide extent. That from 1717 on, the Grand Lodge, selecting a portion only of this store, gradually evolved a Rite consisting of E.A., F.C., M.M., and R.A. That the restriction of the terms "pure," "ancient," and (in a certain sense) "Craft" to the degrees included in this Rite is arbitrary and due solely to the accident of selection by the Grand Lodge.

2. That the earliest additional degrees were founded on other portions of the same esoteric legendary store, that they were founded by Britons, and are as much a British institution as the Grand Lodge Rite itself. That they are therefore entitled to recognition as a part of "pure and ancient Masonry."

3. That there is no evidence of any additional degrees of foreign (i.e., non-British) origin.

d'Alviella Adds Agreement

Commenting on Brother Tuckett's contentions, Count Goblet d'Alviella, then the Grand Commander of the Supreme Council for Belgium, declared: "I quite agree with him (Tuckett) that these degrees, especially the oldest Scottish (Ecossais) Degrees, did not originate on the continent but are a genuine product of British soil, and that while they received their principal extensions after 1740 in France and Germany, their first appearance must be looked for sometime earlier among the British lodges."

Throughout his paper Brother Tuckett stresses that "Scots Mason," "Scots Master," "Scots Masonry," are identical with "Macon Ecossois," "Maitre Ecossois," "Maconnerie Ecossoise" and he goes on to list the following proven items of frequent activities of Ecossais Masonry in England as early or earlier than it appeared on the continent:

BRITISH REFERENCES

1733—Rawlinson's manuscript at the Bodleian (Oxford) includes a list of lodges of the year 1733 which contains "115 Devil Tavern Temple Bar, a 'Scotch Masons Lodge.'"

1734—Pines' engraved list of lodges contains "115 (figure of Devil) 'Scott's Masons Lodge,' Devil, Temple Bar, 2d and 4th Munday."

1735—The Pocket Companion has a similar entry. This lodge continued to meet at the Devil until 1736 when it moved to Daniel's Coffee House and was erased in 1736.

Tuckett then goes on to say, "That it (Devil's Temple Bar Lodge) worked Scots, i.e., Ecossois Masonry will not nowadays be doubted."

1735—Scots Masonry at Bath, October 28, 1735, on this "same day the lodge met extraordinary." Ten were made and admitted "Scots Master Masons." (Min. of R. Cumberland L. Bath.) From the transactions of Somerset Masters Lodge, 1917, appearing in an article entitled "Masonic Lodges of Bath" by G. Norman.

SCOTS' MASTER REFERENCES

Of the ten receiving the degree of Scots Master, two of them had the Degree of Master Mason conferred upon them on the same day, apparently to enable them to proceed to the Degree of Scots Master; thus once again we have definite proof that the degree referred to must have been Ecossais, since it certainly was not the regular Master Mason Degree.

1740—Scots Masonry at Lodge of Antiquity. Nine made "Scotch Master Masons" at an "audit" meeting in a regular lodge. The degrees were conferred by Brother Humphreys of the Morning Bush, Aldersgate. This item is extracted from the records of Lodge of Antiquity under date of June 17, 1740.

1746—Scots Masonry at Salisbury, "October 19, 1746. At this lodge were made 'Scotts Masons' five brethren of the lodge." —G. H. Goldney, "Hist. of F.M. in Wilts.," page 101.

1746—January 8—Scots Masonry at Bath, Bros. Thomas Naish and John Burge are this day made Scotch Masters and paid for making 2s 6d each.—Min. of R. Cumberland L., Bath.

Before we leave Britain and look at the European scene during the near mid-eighteenth century, we should take note of the minutes of two English Lodges, both of which met rather close to the Scottish border.

Gateshead Records

The records of "Lodge of Industry," Swallwell, Gateshead, mention that on July 1, 1746, the "dignity of a Highrodian" and other singular Degrees were conferred. Another lodge close by records that the grade of Harodim (conferred after the 3° and before the R.A.) appears in the minutes of No. 94, Sunderland, December 1, 1756, and many times thereafter as noted by Brother Robert Hudson in his "Origin of the English Rite," 1884, which deals somewhat fully with the additional degrees, but which he stresses came to the notice of Masonic historians sometime after the advent of the Royal Order of Scotland.

FOREIGN REFERENCES

1733—Grade of "Ecossois" in Belgium.—P. Duchaine in La F.M. Belge XVIII Siecle, p. 136.

1737—Documents published in 1892 from the archives of the Grand Lodge of Sweden state that Baron Scheffer received at Paris in 1737 at the hands of Lord Radcliffe (5th Earl of Derwentwater) two "Ecossois Degrees."—(Gould, Concise History, p. 379.)

1741—A "Scots Lodge" at Berlin, Germany.

Brother Tuckett then goes on to say, "These are the earliest Ecossois notices which have been traced. If they are not identical, then the identity in names and dates is simply astounding."

It is interesting to note that the seal of the Charleston, South Carolina Lodge of Perfection established in 1783 bears the name "Sublime Scotch Lodge, Charleston, So. Carolina" and thus shows that it was the founders' intent to adhere to the traditional designation established in London as early as 1733 and carefully followed by all similar organizations during the 18th century.

Expand High Degrees Abroad

In conclusion Brother Tuckett declared, "This review of the evidence points out that the institution of Masonic Degrees or ceremonies outside, beyond or additional to what we now call the Craft was not the work of foreigners but of Britons. Granted that later (much later) the 'High Degree' movement abroad amongst foreign brethren attained dimensions far greater than it ever did at any time with our own countrymen (British) whether at home or in exile, still the beginnings took place in England or Scotland where such degrees were in existence even before Freemasonry had been carried by Britons into France. . . . While this hearty infant—the 3rd degree—was being born and nursed into vigor and general recognition, many others based upon other portions of the same legendary store were being brought into the world, some doubtless still-born, some doomed to perish in infancy, while others were destined to thrive and survive . . ."

18th Century Bordeaux Letters

Interesting additional support to the thinking that the early Ecossais Degrees had their origin in Britain is to be found in one of the Sharp-Bordeaux 18th century Masonic manuscripts. It relates that a certain Brother Dutilles had received his version of the Ecossais Degrees from Admiral Mathews "in company with some foreigners." Writing to Feuillard, Bordeaux' Deputy, under date of April 21, 1746, Dutilles requested instruction in the true Ecossisme. (Sharp-Bordeaux Document No. 3.)

We are of the opinion that the Mathews referred to could only have been the British Vice-Admiral of that name who was then seeing service along the French coast. A Feuilard letter (Sharp-Bordeaux Document No. 4) written to Bordeaux November 9, 1747, states that the Ecossais Degrees conferred by Britain's Admiral Matthews were "well proficient that I could not but recognize him."

Scots Master Ritual

Even as we type these opinions relative to the Genesis of Ecossais Masonry, painstaking and constant research is adding to our store of early data and an important recent ritual discovery tends to bear out the conclusions thus far arrived at.

Lt. Col. Eric Ward, Past Master of Lodge No. 7356, presented two papers during 1962 to England's Premier Lodge of Masonic Research, Quatuor Coronati No. 2076 of London, of which he was Master in 1964. Both papers discuss Early Masters' Lodges and have been incorporated in the Transactions of the Lodge for that year. The papers are factual and the conclusions expressed therein are difficult to refute. The Ward material begins on page 124 and, including many pages of scholarly discussion, ends on page 181.

In commenting upon the situation in France, Brother Ward states that the formation of the first lodge in Paris "soon produced two kinds of Masonry existing side by side . . . a Frankish system restoring the true secrets and superimposing upon the Anglican grades additional degrees each more colorful and splendid than its predecessor . . ."

Crusaders Link K.S. Temple

"Out of this urge to develop a national style came the need for legends transcending in age and splendor the simple unsophisticated material which the English made do, and what was more logical than a direct link with Solomon's Temple through the Christian Crusaders whose last remaining outpost was believed to be in Scotland in which country alone genuine Masonic-cum-chivalric secrets had been so religiously preserved through the ages. So Ecossais Masonry came into being . . . safe in the knowledge that in their day they were too distant from the mystical source to be checked."

An especially important discovery has been made of a Scots Master Ritual which has long reposed in the archives of England's Pilgrim Lodge No. 238, which for years worked in German and boasted of the Duke of Sussex as Master. It is printed in German and according to Ward is based upon a French version of an adapted English Craft Ritual and he goes on to say that the Ritual is "so simple and free from elaboration as to suggest an origin not far removed from 1740."

Wardens in West

In discussing the ritual and its preamble, Col. Ward leaves with us the thought that appropriately enough it might indeed be truly a Scottish Ritual, since the work was conferred in a lodge room formed identically like all Scottish lodges of the 17th and 18th centuries—a form which is still used by many of Scotland's older lodges and which places both Wardens in the West.

Another similarity to Scottish procedure and custom is to be found in the preamble, which states that the lodge is marked out in green and the aprons are lined with green taffeta. Green is still the color used by Scotland for all Grand Lodge regalia.

Col. Ward comments on and quotes from the Scots Master Ritual, in part, as follows:

"The candidate is then informed that he has been called to account for his actions and, having been tried and proved guilty, must expect the reward for his misdeeds. The J.W. is instructed to seize the candidate, turn him 'round, make him sit reversed on a stool, bind his hands together behind his back and place a rope about his neck. The W.M. then announces that this is the ruffian who has slain our Master (i.e., Hiram) and ought to be punished, but because of his knowledge the Order will show mercy. He is therefore released, and the W.M. reads the Oath, of which the following is approximately the English equivalent:—

PLEDGE OF ADMISSION

'I, N.N., swear in the presence of the living God, and in this worthy assembly of Scots Masters, that I will preserve inviolably the secrets of Scots Masonry, and that neither intentionally nor through carelessness will I betray them to a living soul. That I am willing to fulfill to the best of my ability all duties which are demanded of me as a Scots Master, and that I will render the high Scottish Lodge all due obedience. Should I at any time act otherwise, then I shall submit myself to the same penalty to which I was pledged on admission to this high order. So help me God.'

". . . Then he gives him the sign (as if he were about to grasp him,' makes him stand on his right and gives him the grip, thus:—

'The right hand is placed under the elbow of the other, foot to foot and knee to knee; the left hand is put on the right shoulder of the other, saying the word JEHOVA and adding, This is the eternal fighting word and the name of the Lord under whose banner we fight.'

DISPLAYS FLOOR CLOTH

". . . The Master then explains the qualities of a Scots Master, which the ritual states are as difficult as they are different, even though they are insufficient to instruct upon the real purpose of the Order. The qualities demanded of a Scots Master are symbolized by the four animals depicted upon the floor cloth—the Lion (intrepidity, etc.), the Fox (shrewdness), the Ape (emulation), and the Sparrowhawk (alertness), all of which it must be noted also have qualities that must be guarded against."

Col. Ward then adds the following notation: "The use of symbolic animals and birds is possibly a parallel to the Lion, Ox, Man, and Eagle of the 'Antients' Armorial Bearings depicted in Ahiman

Rezon, 1764." (Laurence Dermott's name for the "Antients'" Constitutions.)

Discover D'Assigny Pedigree

In retrospect, it is evident that W. J. Chetwode Crawley, the famed Irish Masonic historian, in his 1896 "Caementaria Hibernica, Fasciculus Secundus," did more to tie together the motivating factors which led up to the creation by Dr. Fifield D'Assigny of his "Serious and Impartial Enquiry into the Cause of the present Decay of Free-Masonry in the Kingdom of Ireland," published in Dublin, Ireland, in 1744.

We say this advisedly, since up to that time the family and personality of Fifield D'Assigny baffled all scrutiny. Though the book was published in Dublin and the author's name was the most unusual in Ireland, no mention of pedigree or his social environment was to be found. Crawley had the good fortune to come across some traces of D'Assigny's career and to identify his family. From his scrutiny we glean the following.

First D'Assigny Generation

The first appearance of the name D'Assigny (or Dassigny or d'Assigny, as the name was variously spelled) in the British Isles is Pierre D'Assigny, a Walloon monk and a convert to the Protestant faith. He appears in London in 1636 and again in Jersey in 1638, where he was Rector of St. Heliers. In 1643 he returned to England and in 1645 turned up at Norwich, where he stirred up strife, and after six years of incessant broils, he returned in 1651 to Jersey. He appears to have been unscrupulous and aggressive and earned the reputation of being an unprincipled schemer. With the restoration of Charles II, he disappeared.

Before obtaining the Rectory of St. Heliers, Pierre D'Assigny had married Elizabeth Marie and became the father of at least two children. The son, born in 1643, was named Marie, after the surname of his mother's family. He Latinized Marie into Marius, entered the English Church, and wrote several theological works of considerable merit, one of which won him the approval of Dr. Samuel Johnson. After the Restoration Marius had sufficient influence to obtain a Royal letter directing the University of Cambridge to confer upon him the degree of S.T.B. (B.D.), although he does not appear to have been a College man. He died November 14, 1717, at the age of 74 and was buried in Essex.

Second Generation

After the death of his first wife, Pierre D'Assigny is known to have married again, although his second wife's name is unknown. By this marriage he had a son, Samuel, who became a notorious figure in Dublin. He comes to light in that city in 1698, established as a cleric, although there is no evidence that he was entitled to use the garb. He published a violent Calvinistic polemic, of which a copy is preserved in the Library of Trinity College, Dublin. The title page reads as follows: "An antidote against the Erroneous, or rather Blasphemous, Opinions of some People in this our Corrupt Age; Concerning the True and Real Cause of Man's falling into those Gross and Notorious Sins, which do commonly prove his Eternal Ruine." He took up the profession of "Couple-beggar," or celebrant of unlicensed marriages, and although he apparently was never in Holy Orders, he wore a Band and a Gown, etc., and so imposed on credulous and hasty lovers.

Imprison Samuel

In 1732 he was imprisoned on a charge of having celebrated a clandestine marriage, but was acquitted. He died five years later and is described as having left effects to "near a Thousand Pounds." Combining his father's aggressive energy with a little of his brother's bent for learning, he was an able man, but his talents were misdirected.

Fifield, Son of Samuel

Fifield D'Assigny, the author of the famous pamphlet, was the son of Samuel, born in 1701. He adopted the medical profession and was a popular practitioner amongst the poorer people of Dublin. There is no trace of his having earned a medical degree or even a license in medicine, and the imposing array of letters after his name on the title page of the newly discovered copy of the "Impartial Answer" is rather difficult to interpret. One of the chief authorities on the history of medicine in Ireland suggests that the letters

"A.S.L.L.S." may mean Apothecary Society Licentiate and Licentiate in Surgery.

He seems to have belonged to the class of roistering free-livers who were aptly described by Laurence Dermott as "joyous companions" who attached themselves to Freemasonry on its convivial side. We can hardly do him an injustice in this estimate of his personality, for we have proof of his mode of life and he appears occasionally in Irish Law Court records. On July 30, 1739, he filed a Bill in Chancery, seeking relief from certain promissory notes which, he alleged, had been extorted from him by threats and violence.

Fifield D'Assigny Complains

The circumstances are so strange that we reproduce his statement here:

> Fifield D'Assigny of Dublin Doctor of Physic complains that about the 21st March 1738, he being then resident in Fleet Street, Dublin, one Wm. Ryan constable came to his lodgings with a Warrant of the Lord Mayor, at suit of Charles Clark, Barrack St., victualler, for a Debt, and forced him to go to said Clark's House: there Clark, Judith his wife and Wm. Ryan locked him up, and on being asked their authority, they produced a book with several charges for rum and other liquors, amounting to £10. They then demanded promissory notes for the amount and threatened if he did not sign them, they would send him to Newgate. He continued in close keeping the greater part of the day, and fearing bodily harm, at last executed the notes. 15/- were then demanded, being said Wm. Ryan's fee for apprehending him to be paid said Wm. Ryan. Terrified at this cruel and unjust behaviour he perfected another note for this amount.

The reply to this bill is equally suggestive:

> Deft. Judith Clark says that in 1737 before her marriage with sd. Clark She from time to time lent and advanced to Compt. for his support and to supply his then great wants several sums of ready money up to £9 12 3 and that he had from Deft. to the value of 11s. 7½d. in liquor. Compt. often ill-treated and abused Deft. Judith. He had agreed to account and offered to pay by instalments.

Append Schedule of Particulars

To this was appended a schedule of particulars, ending with the curious statement:

Defts. deny they ever gave out the debt was for woollen cloth and wearing apparel.

Very shortly after the publication of the "Enquiry" the curtain rises on the last scene of Fifield D'Assigny's chequered life drama. He died in the 37th year of his age, of dropsy, an untimely fate sadly consistent with the excesses of his life.

Whatever may have been the vicissitudes of his career, Fifield D'Assigny had so comported himself that his funeral partook of the character of a public ceremony. The pomp and circumstance attending his obsequies are so quaintly and so strikingly chronicled in newspapers of the time we transcribe the account in full:

IMPRESSIVE FUNERAL DETAILS

Last Thursday (January 10, 1744-45), died Dr. Fifield Designy, who was interred the Sunday following. The Funeral was as follows. 1. The Beadle of the Parish, with conductors and the Tylers of Lodges two and two. 2. The Corps, supported by six Master Masons, properly cloathed. 3. Twelve Mourners, two and two. 4. Six Serjeants of the Foot, in their Regimentals, and proper cloathing. 5. Two Deacons. 6. A Master Mason, with his entered apprentice, two wardens, and a number of the craft, all properly cloathed, two and two. He was a loving friend true to his trust and a gentleman always ready to do his duty, in attending the poor and ordering such medicines as he thought requisite to preserve life, which made his death greatly lamented.

The curt entry of his burial in the Parochial Register of St. Werburgh's, Dublin, runs as follows:

Jan: 13, 1744, Fifield D'Assigny, Wer: Street, aged 36, Dropsy.

The presence amongst the mourners of "Six Serjeants of the Foot, in their Regimentals, and proper cloathing" is not readily explained. We can only venture the surmise that Fifield D'Assigny had been connected in some fashion with the medical staff of the Army. Though we have been unable to trace him in the sparse military records that now survive, the surmise is supported by the fact that St. Werburgh's is, and was, the parish which includes the Castle of Dublin with its military appendages. If he were a Surgeon or an Apothecary to the Forces quartered within its precincts, St. Werburgh's Churchyard would be his natural burial place.

Nothing we know of D'Assigny's life redounds so much to his

credit as the account of his funeral, with its varied band of mourners, civil and military, amongst whom the members of the Fraternity were so conspicuous. Faults no doubt he had, the faults of his day and generation, but the man must have had sterling merits. "He was a loving friend, true to his trust." Is there a Brother amongst us who would not be proud of this epitaph?

A
Serious and Impartial
ENQUIRY
Into the Cause of the present Decay of
FREE-MASONRY
IN THE
Kingdom of *IRELAND*.

Humbly Address'd to all the BRE-
THREN Accepted of before and
since the *Constitutions*.

To which are added,

Such Instructive Remarks as may be
found useful to Revive the Honour of that AN-
TIENT CRAFT.

As likewise, by way of APPENDIX, will be inserted
the OLD and NEW REGULATIONS of the *London*
CONSTITUTIONS, by the Consent and Approbation of the GRAND-LODGE of *Ireland*,
and Dedicated to the Right Worshipful and Right
Hon. the Lord Viscount ALLEN, Grand-Master
of this Kingdom.

The Whole adorned with a Curious Copper-Plate
suitable to the Order and Design.

By Fifield Dassigny, M.D. *Author of the Impartial
Answer to the Enemies of* FREE-MASONS.

DUBLIN:
Printed by EDWARD BATE in *George's-Lane* near
Dame-Street. M,DCC,XLIV.

Title-Page of D'Assigny's *A Serious and Impartial
Enquiry . . .*, 1744.

To the most Noble and Puissant PRINCE

TRUTH.

Dread Sir,

YOUR excellent Wisdom in distinguishing Sincerity from Falshood, in discovering the Base and Impure from the Generous and Brave, emboldens me at this Time to lay before your Feet the following Enquiry; nor will I doubt your Royal Favour, since I have endeavoured to preserve those lasting and unalterable Principles which the Subjects of your Kingdom so remarkably possess; and notwithstanding that the deepest Arts have been contriv'd, the most subtile Machinations formed to overpower and destroy your Territories, to punish and oppress your stedfast and faithful Servants, you have hitherto had the Pleasure to reflect, that all their barbarous and wicked Contrivances have met with a just Disappointment: Nay, Time, that general Depopulator of all other Provinces, hath shewn so eminent a Regard to your Government, that it hath brought to light the cruel Intentions of your Enemies, whereby you have been able to overturn their iniquitous Schemes; and as the Palm-tree, tho' depress'd, with greater Glory Shone.

Thus may you live, most noble Prince, inheriting the Virtues and Honours of your Ancestors, insomuch that Tyranny, Faction, and Depravity of Nature, may at all Seasons submit, and pay due Homage to your Power. I am,

Dread Sir,

Your faithful Subject

and Servant,

The AUTHOR.

PREFACE.

No government can properly subsist without certain wholesome laws and regulations, and as our commonwealth not only pleads the pride of antiquity, but with equal justice boasts of the beauty, order, regularity, and happy disposition of its fundamental constitutions, and as the happiness of the craft also depends on a perfect intimacy with those rules handed down to us by our wise legislators, whose labours and skill, in the everlasting art of Architecture, will demand the praise and admiration of the learned brethren in future ages, I have endeavoured in the following sheets to represent some mistakes, irregularities, and unseemly transactions, which have been occasioned by the want of an acquaintance with them; nor will the brethren, I hope, take it a miss, (as I have chose Truth for my patron) that I should strictly adhere to its principles, and point out the base and impure from the generous and brave's neither is it to be wondered at, that there are some of the former disposition amongst us, since experience evidently convinces that in all sects of men some impious and turbulent spirits appear, whose unlawful actions ought rather to be exposed than concealed, that they themselves may see their evil deeds in a proper light, and turn from their iniquities: where such may be found belonging to our order, I have attempted, by cordial advice, to admonish and rouse them up from their fallen-state insomuch that they may not at any time wander from the paths of virtue, but enjoy fully with the true brethren the lasting relish of its ever-pleasing fountain. Then will they meet with the reward of their Labours, be countenanced and approved of by their lords and masters, and like profitable and worthy servants meet with a general esteem from all mankind.

PREFACE.

The *old and new regulations of the* London *constitutions have, by the worshipful secretary, been carefully transcribed and adapted to the regulations of the Grand Lodge of this kingdom, which will prove of general use to the brethren, who may hereafter have the honour of becoming members of that august assembly, and that my attempts to increase their wellfare may not be fruitless, but meet with the intended success, I heartily implore from him alone who is able to grant my boon, and from whom I also crave that perfectness, plenty, peace, and unanimity, may crown the brethren's days, so that this life ended, they may receive the recompence of their toils, and dwell in the presence of that immortal stone belonging to our building, even the* Alpha *and* Omega *of our redemption.*

A Serious and Impartial

ENQUIRY

Into the Cause of the present Decay of

FREE-MASONRY.

Brethren,

IT is with the utmost anxiety of mind that I have any occasion to employ my pen in representing the decay of Free-masonry; the increase of its wellfare and advancement would have been a more pleasing task to me, but as the design of the present labour is to promote the latter, I shall proceed to make the following enquiries.

First, When or at what time the craft of Freemasonry was instituted.

Secondly, The cause or motive of its Institution.

Thirdly, The qualities or principles of the Craft.

Fourthly, The benefits arising from a strict observance of the principles thereof.

In order to solve the first question, 'twill be necessary to trace antiquity, even unto its infant state, and take a view of our parent

Adam in his sylvan lodge, where the Almighty Architect imprinted on the very tablets of his heart the amazing symmetry and silent harmony of Geometrical proportion—with these principles our Primogenitor readily instructed his offspring, well knowing that they were absolutely essential to the discovery of the secret powers of nature; into whose adamantine gates, when once entered, we are struck with admiration at the wisdom, strength, and beauty of its great Creator. *Cain*, inspired with his father's knowledge, soon erected a fair city and called it after the name of his eldest son *Enoch*, whose posterity daily improved in the discovery and cultivation of various arts, as the way of working in metal, the surprising harmony and modulation of sounds in musick, husbandry, tent making, and formation of structures in stone and timber. *Enoch* (who by gift of prophecy foretold the deluge, and that great day yet to come of final conflagration) formed two pillars, the one made of brick, the other of stone, whereon he engraved the liberal arts and sciences, in order to preserve them from the implacable fury of the mighty waters, or the irresistible force of elements on fire.

Noah and his three sons, by the skill they had in geometrical masonry, and by the power of divine inspiration, built for themselves and their families a wooden world, which saved the faithful from the impending destruction.

In *Shinar's* plain the masons next appeared, who fraught with vain ambitious views of forming unto themselves a name, laid the foundation of *Babel's* stupendous tower which they intended should reach the summit of *Æther's* wide expanse; but the Omniscient Power (whose edicts none dare dispute) thought it necessary to curb the pride of haughty man, and marr their grand design, for when they had rais'd the building to a prodigious height, having spent 53 years labour therein, he caused their lips to loose their usual sounds, and made each language flow in confus'd terms: yet still the faithful preserved their sacred mysteries, and formed a compact amongst themselves to hand them down to their successors, which valuable priviledges we are possessors of at this time.

The confusion of tongues did not obstruct the improvement of the royal art; for *Nimrod*, who founded the *Assyrian* monarchy, built after the general dispersion many famous cities, as *Nineveh*,

Rhohoboth, &c, upon the *Tygris* and *Euphrates* flourished afterwards many learned men, known by the names of *Magi* and *Chaldees*, who being skilful in mathematicks, preserved and adorned that excellent science Geometry, which in succeeding ages became the favorite of royalty and nobility. But of these premises the Craft will receive a clearer information in a formed Lodge. So likewise did the descendants of *Shem Ham* and *Japhet* in their respective colonies, *viz.* in *Asia*, *Africa*, and *Europe*, give undeniable testimonies of their masterly designs, which are sufficient vestiges to demonstrate their skill in Masonry. But of these the *Assyrians* and *Egyptians* made the greatest progress, as *Babylon's* stately walls and the famous *Pyramids* of the latter most evidently prove, and so distinguishable was the early taste and genius of that antient kingdom, that they were justly stiled two of the seven wonders of the universe.

The glorious temple of *Diana* at *Ephesus* next engages our admiration, which was finished by those excellent Master Masons *Dresiphon* and *Archiphron*, and bears the name of the third wonder; nor shall the tomb of *Mausolus* king of *Caria* be passed over in silence, which, together with the temple of *Babylon*, the famous light house, or tower of *Pharos*, and the colossus at *Rhodes*, claim characters not inferior to the rest.

The learned *Abraham* instructed his sons in the *Assyrian* learning, who made no great figure in Architecture while under *Pharaoh's* cruel yoke, or during their peregrination in the desarts of *Arabia*, until the inspired *Aholiab* and *Bezaleel* erected a most glorious tabernacle, which afterwards proved the model of *Solomon's* temple, according to the pattern which God gave *Moses* in the mount, who then became the Grand Master Mason of the Lodge at *Israel*, and imparted to the *Brethren* such wise charges and orders, that they daily advanced in the art of Geometry and even excelled the *Canaanites*; yet *Dagon's* temple, or the most beautiful structures of *Tyre* and *Sidon* could not equal that stupendous and finished piece, the Temple of the Eternal God, built by the peculiar influence of Heaven, under the direction of that ever memorable Prince of peace and Architecture king *Solomon*, Grand Master of the Lodge at *Jerusalem*, whose father *David* was deprived of that immortal honour because he was unhappily engaged in wars, and seemed fond of destruction, whereby his hands were oft polluted with innocent bloood.

This gorgeous and splendid edifice, fit for the special refulgence of the Almighty Glory, must transcend the utmost bounds of our imagination, for it certainly was the most curious piece of Masonry that ever yet appeared or ever will upon earth; wherefore tis natural to believe, that such a beautifull structure soon engaged artists from all nations to view the excellency of the work, which was carried on by the wisdom and dexterity of the learned *Hiram*, Grand Master of the Lodge of *Tyre*, who together with the inspired *Hiram abif*, Master of the work, without the noise of tools, produced the most perfect pattern of Architecture the wonder and amazment of the travelling world.

Masonry, soon after the erection of *Solomon's* temple, became in a most flourishing condition, and the artists employed in that grand work dispersed themselves thro' all the neighbouring nations, where they instructed the free-born sons of eminent persons in this useful and liberal art, insomuch that kings, princes, and potentates, became Grand Masters in their respective territories; and being filled with a glorious spirit of emulation, they strove to excell each other in improving and advancing the Royal Art.

This wonderful model of workmanship the Temple, in 416 years after being finished, felt the dreadfull effects of war-like rage, and by the absolute and despotick power of that grand monarch *Nebuchadnezar* was reduce to ashes; and tho after a general peace proclaimed, his heart relented and he studied with the utmost diligence the rules of Architecture, and raised several stately piles, yet were they vastly inferior in the sublime perfection of Masonry to the sacred and amiable Temple of God, which still remain'd inimitable.

In the reign of grand *Cyrus* the *Jews*, who were carried captives to *Babylon*, on their return to *Jerusalem* laid the foundation of the second Temple, but that monarch dying before it was finished, the cape stone was put on in the sixth year of *Darius* king of *Persia*, and was dedicated with joy and many large sacrifices by *Zerubbabel*, their prince, and general Master Mason; and tho' this stupendous fabrick came infinitely short of the elegance and order of *Solomon's* temple, yet as it was raised exactly upon his foundation, and according to his model, it must be allowed to be a most regular symmetrical and glorious edifice, as the enemies of the *Jews* have frequently testifyed.

At length the royal art was carried into *Greece* whose inhabitants erected several noble structures, as the citadel of *Athens*, the temples of *Minerva*, *Theseus*, *Jupiter Olympius*, with many other publick halls, palaces, forums, gymnasiums, &c. do sufficiently witness, yet did they not arrive to any considerable knowledge in Geometry until *Thales Milesius*, and his scholar the greater *Pythagorus* appeared, who proved the author of the 47th proposition of *Euclid's* first book; which if rightly understood is the foundation of all Masonry sacred, civil, and military.

Geometry after *Pythagoras* became the darling study of *Greece*, and many learned philosophers arose, who invented sundry propositions and reduced them to the use of the mechanical arts; nor is it to be doubted but Masonry kept pace with that science, or rather followed it in gradual improvements, until the admirable *Euclid* of *Tyre* flourished at *Alexandria*, under the patronage of *Ptolomeus* king of *Ægypt*, who gathered up its scattered elements, and digested into a method not yet excelled, for which laborious undertaking his name will always meet with renown, and his memory be ever green amongst us.

The next king of *Ægypt*, *Ptolomeus Philadelphus*, was a great improver of the liberal arts, as well as of all useful knowledge, who having collected the most curious library upon earth, he caused the old testament to be translated into *Greek*, and became an excellent Architect and General Master Mason.

We have no reason to scruple but that the *African* nations, even unto the *Atlantic* shore, did soon imitate *Ægypt's* improvements, altho' history gives us no light therein, and travellers have not met with encouragment to discover the valuable remains of Masonry in those once renowned nations.

The learned isle of *Sicily* demands our remembrance, for there flourished that prodigious Geometrician *Archimedes*, and the antient *Romans* were obliged to that island, as well as to *Greece*, *Ægypt*, and *Asia*, for their knowledge both in the science and in the art; for when they subdued nations mighty discoveries appeared, and the eminent professors were led captives to *Rome*, which then became the center of learning, and of imperial power, until in the reign of *Augustus Cæsar* they advanced to their zenith of glory, at which time the Messiah came, who proved the great Architect of the church, and caused the uneasy multitude to taste the delicacies of lovely quiet, and to enoy the pleasing advantages of humble peace. In this happy state the Craft had great opportunities in making improvements, and giving due encouragement to their dexterous artists whose learned scholars and pupils, but particularly the great *Vitruvius* the father of all true Architects, erected several sumptuous buildings, which are the standard of Masonry at this day.

Therefore it is rationally believed, that the great *Augustus*, who patronized *Vitruvius*, and promoted the welfare of the fellow Craftsmen was the Grand Master of the Lodge at *Rome*, as appears by the many magnificent structures of his reign, which are an epitome of the *Asiatic*, *Egyptian*, *Grecian*, and *Sicilian* Architecture; and which we often express by the name of the *Augustan* stile, altho' as yet we are only imitators thereof not having arrived to its perfection.

From the beginning of the world the antient records of Masons afford indisputable proofs, that when the civil powers shewed an abhorrence to tyranny and slavery, and the bright and free genius of the Craftsmen had due scope, that then above all other artists they were the favourites of the most eminent who protected them in order to carry on their grand undertakings. Nor should it be forgot that all Craftsmen, who work by Geometrical Rules of building, deserve to be called good Masons as well painters, statuaries, as stone cutters, bricklayers, carpenters, &c. tho no age hath since been adorned with a man so well versed in cunning in all parts of Masonry, as the renowned *Hiram abif*.

While the *Roman* empire continued in its glory, the Royal art was carefully propagated, even to the *Ultima Thule* and a Lodge erected in almost every *Roman* garrison, whereby they generously communicated their cunning to the nothern and western parts of *Europe*, which had grown barbarous before the *Roman* conquest; there being but few remains of good Masonry before that period.

But when the *Goths* and *Vandals*, who had never been conquered by the *Romans*, like a general deluge overspread the *Roman* empire, with warlike rage and gross ignorance, few of their finished edifices escaped from being either defaced or totally destroyed.

The *Asiatic* and *African* nations, felt the weight of the same calamity by the conquest of the *Mahometans*, who in stead of cultivating the arts and sciences, designed to convert the world by the cruel method of fire and sword.

Thus upon the declension of the *Roman* empire, when the *British* garrisons were raised, the *Angles* and other lower *Saxons* being invited by the antient *Britons* to come over and help them against the *Scots* and *Picts*, who being related to the *Goths*, or rather a sort of *Vandals*, possessed with the same warlike disposition and heathenish ignorance, encouraged nothing but war until they were converted into christianity, when they had cause to lament, tho' too late, the gross ignorance of their fathers, in the loss of *Roman* Masonry, which they knew not how to repair. But becoming a free people (as the old *Saxon* laws testify) and having a disposition for Masonry, they soon began to imitate the *Asiatics*, *Grecians*, and *Romans*, in erecting of Lodges, and giving encouragement to Masons, being taught not only from the faithful tradition and valuable remains of the *Britons* but even by foreign princes, in whose dominions the Royal Art hath been much preserved from *Gothic* ruins; particularly by *Charles Martell* king of *France*, who according to the old records of Masonry, sent over several expert Craftsmen and learned Architects into *England*, at the request of the *Saxon* kings, so that during the Heptarchy the *Gothic* Architecture was as much encouraged here as in other christian lands.

And tho' the invasion of the *Danes* occasioned the loss of some records, yet many venerable *Gothic* buildings remained; and after the *Saxons* and *Danes* were conquered by the *Normans*, *Gothic* Masonry was mightily encouraged even by *William* the conqueror, who built the tower of London, and many strong castles and religious edifices. His son *William Rufus* also built *Westminster Hall*, which is reputed to be the largest room upon earth.

Nor did the *Barons* wars or those of the subsequent *Norman* kings, and their contending branches, in any great measure hinder the clergy, or those who enjoy'd large revenues, from raising sumptuous and lofty buildings, for king *Edward* III. had an officer called the kings Free Mason, who was employed to survey all his buildings, and did erect several abbeys, &c. but for the better instruction of candidates and younger Brethren, a certain record of

Free Masonry, written in the reign of king *Edward* IV. gives the following authentick account, *viz.*:

> "That tho' the antient records of the Brotherhood in *England* were many of them destroyed in the wars of the *Saxons* and *Danes*, yet king *Athelstan* (the grandson of king *Alfred* the great, a mighty Architect) the first anointed king of *England*, and who translated the holy Bible into the *Saxon* tongue when he had brought the land into rest and peace, built many great works, and encouraged many Masons from *France*, who were appointed overseers thereof, and brought with them the charges and regulations of the Lodges preserved since the *Roman* times who also prevailed with the king to improve the constitution of the Lodges according to the foreign model, and to increase the wages of working Masons. That the said kings youngest son, prince *Edwin*, being taught Masonry, and taking upon him the charges of a Master Mason, for the love he had to the said Craft, and the honourable principles whereon it is grounded, purchased a free Charter of king *Athelstan*, his father, for the Masons having a correction amongst themselves (as it was antiently expressed) or a freedom and power to regulate themselves, to amend what might happen amiss, and to hold a yearly communication and general assembly.
>
> That accordingly prince *Edwin* summoned all the Masons in the realm to meet him in a congregation at *York*, * who came and composed a General Lodge, of which he was Grand Master, and having brought with them all the writings and records extant, which were in *Greek, Latin, French,* and other languages, from the contents thereof they framed the constitutions and charges of a Lodge, made a law to preserve and observe the fame in all time coming, and ordained good pay for working Masons, &c. *Hal.*
>
> That in process of time when Lodges became numerous, the right worshipful the Master and Fellows, with consent of the Lords of the realm, (for most great men were then Masons) ordained, that for the future at the making or admission of a Brother, the constitution should be read, and the charges hereunto annexed by the Master or Warden, and that such as were to be admitted Master Masons, or Masters of the work should be examined whether they be able of cunning to serve their respective Lords, as well the lowest as the highest, to the honour and worship of the aforesaid art, and to the

---

* *I am informed in that city is held an assembly of Master Masons under the title of Royal Arch Masons, who as their qualifications and excellencies are superior to others they receive a larger pay than working Masons; but of this more hereafter.*

profit of their Lords; for they be their Lords who pay them for their service and travel.

"And besides many other things the said record adds, that those charges and laws of Free Masons have been seen and perused by our late sovereign king *Henry* VI. and by the lords of his honourable council, who have allowed them, and said that they be good right and reasonable to be holden as they have been drawn out and collected from the records of antient times.*

Now although in the reign of King *Henry* VI. while an infant, a certain act of parliament passed affecting only the working Masons, who had contrary to the statutes for labourers combined together not to work, but at their own prices, yet as it was supposed that such confederacies were formed in the general Lodges, they thought it expedient to level the said act against Masons, holding themselves in chapters and congregations†. But when the said king arrived to man's estate, and the records and charges were laid before him and some of his lords (who then must have incorporated themselves with that antient fraternity) they were solemnly approved of as good and fit to be holden.

But as there was not a single instance of the act's being put into execution in that or any other reign, the brethren continued to

---

* *In another manuscript more antient we read, that when the Master and Wardens meet in a Lodge, if need be, the sheriff of the county, mayor of the city or an alderman of the town, in which the congregation is held, should be made fellow and sociate to the Master, in help of him against rebells and for upbearing the rights of the realm.*

That entered apprentices at their making were charged not to be thieves, or thieves maintainers, that they should travel honestly for their pay, and love their fellows as themselves, and be true to the King of England, *to the realm and to the Lodge.*

That at such congregations it shall be enquired, whether any Master or Fellow hath broke any of the articles agreed to; and if the offender, being duly cited to appear, prove rebel and will not attend, then the Lodge shall determine against him that he shall forswear or renounce his Masonry, and shall no more use this Craft, the which if he presume for to do, the sheriff of the county shall imprison him and take all his goods into the Kings hands till his grace be granted him and issued: for this cause principally have these congregations been ordained, that as well the lowest as the highest should be well and truly served in the art aforesaid throughout the kingdom. Amen so mote it be.

† *Tertie Henrici* vi. *Cap.* 1. *An Dom* 1425. *Co sust* 3. *p.* 99.

hold their Lodges, and thought it not worth their while to employ their noble and eminent Brethren to have it repealed; because working Masons, who are free of a Lodge, scorn to be guilty of any combination, and others accepted Masons have no concern in trespases against statutes for labourers *.

The kings of *Scotland* very much encouraged the Royal Art, from the earliest time down to the union of the crowns, where Lodges were kept up without interruption, whose records testify the great regard those Kings paid to the honourable fraternity, who always gave undeniable evidencies of their love and loyalty, from whence sprung the old toast amongst *Scots* Masons, *viz.* GOD *Bless the King and the Craft.* This royal example was followed by the nobility, gentry, and clergy, of *Scotland,* who with the utmost assiduity joined in the promotion of the Craft and Brotherhood, and so great a deference was paid to that noble order, that the Grand Master and Warden received an annual stipend from the crown as also an acknowledgment from every new Brother in the kingdom at entrance, who had power not only to regulate whatever might happen amiss in the brotherhood, but also to hear and finally determine all controversies between Mason and Lord, to punish the Mason if he deserved it, and to oblige both to equitable terms; and this privilege remained until the unfortunate civil wars, yet the great care the *Scots* took to preserve true Masonry proved afterwards very advantageous to *England.*

The learned and magnanimous Queen *Elizabeth* beginning her reign in troublesome times, was diffident of her subjects holding

---

* *It is to be remarked that this act was formed when solid learning was a crime, and Geometry condemned for conjuration; wherefore the ignorance of these times are so apparent, that tradition informs us that the parliamentmen were influenced by the illiterate clergy, who understood neither the secrets of the Craft, nor true Architecture; but apprehending that they had an indefeasible right to the secrets of the people by auricular confession, were strongly disgusted that the Masons should preserve their Grand benefits and valuable priviledges from them; whereupon they represented them as dangerous to the state, and artfully perswaded the members of both houses to make an act which might reflect dishonour even upon the whole Fraternity. But the opinion of the great judge Coke* clears all our daubts in regard to the statute against Masons.*

* *Vide Co. inst part* 3. *fol* 99.

private assemblies, she therefore attempted to dissolve the annual communication of Free-Masonry, as dangerous to her government and being a woman, could not be introduced into the fraternity; but she thought it necessary to commission some noble persons to pay a visit to the Lodge at *York*, where being admitted, they threw aside their arms and returned the Queen a most honourable account of the antient fraternity, whereby her political fears and doubts were removed, and she let them alone as a people much respected by the noble and wise of all political nations.

Upon her demise king *James* the VI. of *Scotland* succeeding to the crown of *England*, (who was a Mason *King*) revived the *English* Lodges, and as he was the first king of *Great Britain*, he was also the first prince in the world that recovered the *Roman* Architecture from the ruins of *Gothick* ignorance. For after many illiterate ages, when learning again its drooping head uplifted, and the science of Geometry recovered its ground, the polite nations then began to discover the confusion and impropriety of the *Gothick* Buildings, and in the 15 and 16 centuries the *Augustan* stile was raised from its rubbish in *Italy*, by many bright Architects, but more particularly by the great *Palladio*, who tho' not imitated there, was justly rival'd in *England* by our Great Master Mason *Inigo Jones*.

And notwithstanding all true Masons pay due honour to the memories of those *Italian* Architects, yet the *Augustan* stile was not revived by any crowned head before king *James* the first of *England*, who employed the said glorious *Inigo Jones* to build his royal palace of *White-hall*; and upon that king's demise his son *Charles* the I, being also a Mason king, intended to carry on his royal father's design according to Mr. *Jones*'s stile, but was unhappily diverted by the civil wars, and it is allowed by all skillful Architects, that Master *Jones*'s designs and erections are originals, and at first view discover his mighty genius in Architecture, for which he was as much honoured by the nobility and gentry of *Scotland* as of *England*.

Masonry could not help feeling the dismal effects of the wars in those times, but when the royal family was restored and a general peace proclaimed throughout the nation, it then began to flourish again, as appears by the productions of Sr. *Christopher*

Wren and Sr. *William Bruce*, who followed the inimitable designs of Master *Inigo Jones*.

In the reign of king *James* the II. the Lodges of Free Masonry in *London*, dwindled into ignorance, for want of being duly frequented and properly cultivated; but after the revolution anno 1688, the glorious King *William*, tho' a warlike prince, had an excellent tast of Architecture, which is evidently proved by his carrying on the building of the two famous hospitals, *Greenwich*, and *Chelsea*, together with the palace of *Hampton Court, Loo* in *Holland, &c.* and the bright example of that prince influenced the learned of *Great Britain* to affect the *Augustan* stile, as appears by the stately edifices erected since throughout the kingdoms of *England* and *Ireland*, not only in the reign of her majesty Queen *Anne*, but likewise in that of King *George* the I. and his Royal successor, the present majesty of these Realms, whom GOD long preserve.

To describe the mighty influence of the Craft of Free Masonry in every age, and in every nation since the beginning of the world, would require many volumes; but, were it expedient, it could easily be proved that the knights of *Malta* and many other religious orders and societies, did borrow their solemn usages from our antient fraternity, who can with the utmost truth assert that no set of men can be better instituted, more decently installed, or whose laws and charges in general have been more sacredly observed; and tho' we have maintained and propagated our concernments in a method peculiar to ourselves, which hath hitherto risisted the violent attempts of the most learned and cunning in all ages, who have by several means strove to steal our secrets from us, while neither the loss of speech or the want of knowledge in different languages could prevent us from knowing and loving one another.

Having now described the antiquity of the Royal Art, and the honours paid to the Craftsmen by the learned and noble of all ages (for the most part of which particulars I confess my self indebted to the several tracts of Historical Masonry printed both in *London* and *Dublin*) I shall proceed to enquire into the cause or motive of its institution, which will appear more plain hereafter when we take a view of the principles of the Craft, and the benefits arising from a strict observance thereof; but in the mean time shall inform you that without Masonry the world would have afforded a rude and irregular prospect, and its inhabitants liable to the severity of inclement seasons, to the raging dogstar's heat and piercing cold, to the greedy savage, whose voice in sounds, ungrateful to human ears, thro' all the forest rings, and to the daring insults and bold attempts of aspiring warriors, while by Masons art majestic piles arise to defend mankind, and nature unpolished owns its harmonious and friendly influence. By Masons art religious domes appear, where the Almighty Architect is worshiped in spirit and in truth.

By Masons art the avaritious miser opens his iron bounded breast, and feels compassion's tender warmth.

By Masons art the injurious and unruly tongue falls down before the throne of awful silence; and readily submits to her commands.

By Masons art the wings of loose desire are clipped, and the lascivious mind restrained from all immodest and unlawful bents.

By Masons art the puny fop (mankinds disgrace) rejects a vain and guady outside, and gladly accepts of more valuable and permanent furniture within.

By Masons art ensigns of state and princely ornaments (the nursery of pride, where ambition keeps her lofty seat) as useless toys by free born sons meet with disdain, since they can boast of a more lasting glory who are

Ennobled by the name they bear,

* Distinguished by the badge they wear.

By Masons art impartial justice her equal ballance holds, and fraud oppressive owns her gentle sway.

Since then by this noble art so many extraordinary advantages accrue, I presume it will of consequence be granted, that the wellfare and good of mankind was the cause or motive of so grand an institution (no art yet ever being so extensively useful) which not only tends to protect them from external injuries, but to polish the rusty dispositions of iniquitous minds, and to detain them within the limited and pleasant bounds of true religion, morality and virtue.

In the next place I shall beg leave to treat of the principles of

---

* *Vide fellow Crafts song by Bro. C Delasay, Esq;*

the Craft, which I hope will meet with a just admiration because they are founded upon religion, morality, Brotherly-love, and good fellowship.

A Mason is obliged by his tenure to believe firmly in the true Worship of the Eternal God, as well as in all those sacred records which the dignitaries, fathers, and apostles of the church have compiled and published for the use of christians; so that no one who rightly understands the art can possibly tread in the irreligious paths of the unhappy libertine, or be induced to follow the arrogant professors of atheism or deism; neither is he to be stained with the gross errors of blind superstition, but may have the liberty of embracing what faith he shall think proper, provided at all times he pays a due reverence to his Creator, and by the world deals with honour and honesty, ever making that golden precept the standard rule of his actions, which engages *to do unto all men as he would they should do unto him.* For the Craft, instead of entring into idle and unnecessary disputes, concerning the different opinions and persuasions of men, admits into the fraternity all that are good and true, whereby it hath become the center of union, and hath brought about the means of reconciliation amongst persons, who without that assistance, would have remained at a perpetual variance.

A Mason, as a lover of quiet, is always subject to the civil powers, provided they do not infringe upon the limitted bounds of religion and reason, and it was never yet known that a real Craftsman was concerned in any dark plot, designs or contrivances against the state; because the wellfare of the nation is alone his peculiar care, so that from the highest to the lowest step of magistracy, due regard and deference is paid by him.

But as Masonry hath at several times felt the injurious effects of war, bloodshed and devastation it was a stronger engagement to the Craftsmen to act agreeable to the rules of peace and loyalty, the many proofs of which behaviour, hath occasioned the antient kings and powers to protect and defend them. But if a Brother should be so far unhappily mistaken as to rebel against the state, he would meet with no countenance from his fellows, and tho' he could not for that crime alone be excluded the Lodge, the Brethren would keep no private converse with him, whereby the government might have cause to be jealous or take the least umbrage.

A Mason, in regard to himself, is carefully to avoid all manner of intemperance or excess, which might obstruct him in the performance of the necessary duties of his laudable profession, or lead him into any crimes which would reflect dishonour upon the antient fraternity.

He is to treat his inferiors as he would have his superiors deal with him, wisely considering that the original of all mankind is the same, and tho' Masonry divests no man of his honour, yet does the Craft admit, that strictly to pursue the paths of virtue, whereby a clear conscience may be preserv'd, is the only method to make any man noble.

A Mason is to be so far benevolent as never to shut his ear unkindly to the complaints of wretched poverty, but when a brother is oppressed by want, he is in a peculiar manner to listen to his sufferings with attention, in consequence of which pity must flow from his breath: and relief without prejudice according to his capacity.

A Mason is to pay due obedience to the authority of his master and presiding officers, and to behave himself meekly amongst his fellows, neither neglecting his usual occupation for the sake of Masonry, nor to quarrel with the ignorant multitude for their ridiculous aspersions concerning it, but at his leisure hours he is required to study the arts and sciences with a diligent mind, that he may not only perform his duty to his great Creator, but also to his neighbor and to himself; for to walk humbly in the sight of GOD to do justice and to love mercy are the certain characteristicks of a real Mason, which qualifications I humbly hope they will profess to the end of time, and I dare venture to say that every true Brother will join with me in *Amen*.

The benefits arising from a strict observance of the principles of the Craft are so apparent, that I must believe every christian would be fond to profess and practice the same, because those principles tend to promote the happiness of life as they are founded on the basis of wisdom and virtue.

Now as it is every man's wish and design to accomplish the business of an happy life, how comes it that we see so many fall short of it? the reason I believe will appear conspicuous, when we reflect that the giddy croud which are most numerous, open a beaten tract which their erring and mistaken followers after their mad example, pursue, leaving the light of reason behind them; and as the wise *Seneca* justly observes it fares:

> "with us in human life, as in a routed army, one stumbles first and then another falls upon him, and so they follow one upon the neck of another, till the whole field comes to be but one heap of miscarriages. Wherefore how careful ought we then to be (if happiness is our aim) to leave this croud, for true felicity is not to be found there, but in a sound mind which judges a right and perseveres in such judgment, ever observing a due decorum in our actions and squaring our lives according to the dictates of right reason."

And surely it may engage the admiration of some that a Craft (whose antiquity is from time immemorial, and whose qualification are only provable by the touchstone of true merit) should meet with contempt or fall into decay; but when daily circumstances are evident marks of my assertions, I must with some regret lay open the irregular deeds of mistaken men, and should be well pleased that they, feeling their follies, may no longer continue in them, but rather pursue the antient land marks of our virtuous Brethren.

In the first place as our priviledges and instructions, when rightly made use of, are not only productive of our welfare on this side of the grave, but even our eternal happiness hereafter, they ought to be communicated to those alone who might improve and enhance their value; whereas on the contrary in several Lodges, too many have been fond of a trifling treat, and have sold their birth-rights at a mean price even for a mess of pottage; and instead of taking a due and especial care to enquire into the reputation or character of the candidate, they have imprudently hurried him into the Craft, and that perhaps too at an age before he arrived to mature discretion, or while under bondage and servitude, contrary to the known constitutions.

REMARKS.

That this custom hath been too prevalent, I believe no one who hath been conversant with our Lodges will deny; and it must give pain to every faithful Mason to see the sacred rules of the order profained or broke thro', I shall beg leave to acquaint the Brethren, that all persons admitted members of a Lodge should bear the character of being free in birth and from bonds, for in juvenile years it is not to be expected that any one can be capable to promote the wellfare of the Craft, which is or ought to be the real intention of introducing any member therein, who likewise ought to be without maim or defect, either in body or mind; the former being sufficient to prevent them from serving their Lords and Masters as they ought, and the latter from falling into immoral or scandalous actions, which the Craft, instead of countenancing, ever shewed the utmost abhorrence and detestation thereto.

And from the imprudence of introducing such members, various divisions and disputes have arose in Lodges, where the Brethren (instead of preserving the harmonious and friendly concord that ought to subsist amongst them) have unluckily fell into factious parties; so that unanimity, which ever will be the lasting cement of the Brotherhood, hath been dissolved.

REMARKS.

As an house divided against itself cannot stand, so likewise it is absolutely essential that every community should preserve peace and harmony as the surest foundation of its welfare; and I cannot help expressing my concern to hear of so many idle and trifling disputes as lately have happened amongst some of the fraternity, occasioned, as I must imagine, by the unfortunate and inconsiderate election of their members; the examples of whom ought highly to engage us in a strict examination of the temper, disposition, and conduct of each candidate; for one contentious man may subvert and spoil the peace and quiet of our harmless hours, and as the old Proverb alledges.

> *Unica prava pecus inficet omnia pecus,*
> One scabby sheep may infect an whole flock.

But how ridiculous do partisans concerning religion appear amongst us? Whereas the Craft tho' founded upon that solid basis will admit of no such controversies, and provided we are not all of the same opinion in matters of faith, yet ought we ever to be of one mind in matters of Masonry; that is to labour justly, not to eat any man's bread for nought, but to the utmost of our capacity to love and serve each other, as Brethren of the same household ought to do: nor can I help judging it as great an absurdity in one man to quarrel with another, because he will not believe as he does, as it would be in him to be angry because he was not exactly of the same size and countenance, &c. but the true Brotherhood are resolved never to suffer any trifle to enter into the door of the Lodge upon that or any other point whatsomever.

Some years ago I had the honour to introduce to the Grand Lodge a remonstrance, setting forth the necessity of a strict scrutiny into the candidates behaviour and character, which I humbly proposed should be by their having one months notice and upon receiving such intelligence, they (as having power) should appoint two of their members nicely to examine into the requisites, and tho' that most revered and august assembly did not agree to it at that particular juncture, I cannot help believing it would greatly tend to the honour and welfare of the Craft, and prevent some complaints of which we at present have cause to make mention of; but, however, shall always be fond to leave all matters of consideration to their mature and superior judgment.

The honours due to the Craft forbids me to pass over a certain set of unprofitable labourers, who under a pretense of knowledge in the art, strive to lead astray, after their irregular method, many persons of credit and reputation.

REMARKS.

It is too well known that in this city lately hath appeared a number of mean and low spirited wretches, who, (if ever just) have turned rebels to our well formed Government, and artfully brought into their iniquitous net several unguarded men, who from me shall meet with pity instead of blame (because they knew not the truth) wherefore I shall beg leave to acquaint them, that the laws of our constitution are so agreeable to the disposition of every good man, and so easily performed, that I dare say no one can have an excuse for not obeying; but as these labourers work not to serve our worthy masters, they receive instead of the advantages accruing from our vineyard, the just reward of their actions, and in each honest breath are stigmatized with a name I here shall not mention.

These despicaple traders or hucksters in pretended Masonry, every prudent Brother ought carefully to avoid holding any converse with them; but as that learned apostle, St. *Paul,* in his Epistle to the *Thessalonians,* very justly advises, *Withdraw yourselves from every Brother that walketh disorderly, and not after the tradition which he received of us; for yourselves know how you ought to follow us, behaving orderly amongst you, neither eating any mans bread for nought, nor weary with well doing; but labouring night and day to raise up the fallen, not counting them as enemies, but admonishing them as Brethren.*

This doctrine of our great Apostle is perfectly consentaneous with the principles of the Craft, which commands to shew the utmost abhorrence to all evil, irregular, or unjust actions, to all rude or disorderly methods of behaviour; for as it is observable that a pestilential air may endanger the health of the best constitution, so likewise may the examples of dissolute men stagger and disappoint the designs of the virtuous, yet notwithstanding that we ought to withdraw ourselves from the converse of those engaged in iniquitous practices, we are not entirely to give them up, but to pity them as unhappy and fallen men, who have strayed from the ways of truth and virtue, and who have not followed the tradition which they received from us, nor pursued the equitable dictates of our excellent and antient commonwealth, whose laws are not only easy in their performance, but agreeable to the interest of each individual, and even essentital to future happiness.

Regularity, virtue and concord, are the only ornaments of human nature (which is often too prone to act in different capacities) so that the happiness of life depends in a great measure on our own election, and a prudent choice of those steps, for human society cannot subsist without concord and the maintenance of mutual good offices; for like the working of an arch of stone, it would fall to the ground provided one piece did not properly support another.

Therefore to afford succour to the distressed, to divide our bread with the industrious poor, and to put the misguided traveller into his way, are qualifications inherent in the Craft, and suitable to its dignity, and such as the worthy members of that great body have at all times strove with indefatigable pains to accomplish.

Now as the land marks of the constitution of Free-Masonry are universally the same throughout all kingdoms, and are so well fixt that they will not admit of removal, how comes it to pass that some have been led a way with ridiculous innovations, an example, of which, I shall prove by a certain propagator of a false system some few years ago in this city, who imposed upon several very worthy men under a pretence of being Master of the Royal Arch, which he asserted he had brought with him from the city of *York*; and that the beauties of the Craft did principally consist in the knowledge of this valuable piece of Masonry. However he carried on his scheme for several months, and many of the learned and wise were his followers, till at length his fallacious art was discovered by a Brother of probity and wisdom, who had some small space before attained that excellent part of Masonry in *London* and plainly proved that his doctrine was false; whereupon the Brethren justly despised him and ordered him to be excluded from all benefits of the Craft, and altho' some of the fraternity have expressed an uneasiness at this matter being kept a secret from them (since they had already passed thro' the usual degrees of probation) I cannot help being of opinion, that they have no right to any such benefit until they make a proper application, and are received with due formality, and as it is an organis'd body of men who have passed the chair, and given undeniable proofs of their skill in Architecture, it cannot be treated with too much reverence, and more especially since the characters of the present members of that particular Lodge are untainted, and their behaviour judicious and unexceptionable; so that there cannot be the least hinge to hang a doubt on, but that they are most excellent Masons.

I cannot help informing the Brethren that there is lately arrived in this city a certain intinerant Mason, whose judgment (as he declares) is so far illumin'd, and whose optics are so strong that they can bear the view of the most lucid rays of the sun at noon day, and altho' we have contented ourselves with three material steps to approach our *Summum Bonum*, the immortal GOD, yet he presumes to acquaint us that he can add three more, which when properly plac'd may advance us to the highest heavens.

It is universally allowed, that the *Italians* are excellent Masons, and have produced to the world the most masterly designs, but I cannot be of opinion that their private usuages or customs are different from the general method exhibited throughout all other nations, and I never yet could hear that there was any order in Masonry under that particular denomination of the *Italic* order, until this mighty Architect, or, I may rather say, extravagant climber, came to impart to his countrymen so valuable a production.

For my part I shall always profess a very great esteem for any one who shall add to the beauty of our glorious art, or by any means improve or enhance the value thereof, and were I assured that this adept had skill sufficient to demonstrate the truth of his assertion, I should pay him the utmost veneration; but until then he must excuse me from being one of his devotees, and I hope that no innocent and worthy Brother may at any time be misled by false insinuations, or foreign schemes.

In ancient times Lodges were only schools of Architecture, and the presiding Masters were generally learned geometricans, who took care to instruct their Brethren and fellows in the study of the liberal arts and sciences, and for their better government they formed such laws and general regulations as were thought necessary to maintain the harmony and well being of each particular organiz'd body, and upon the neglect of attendance of either Master or fellow (when duly summoned) a severe censure was incurred, untill he could prove unto the whole Lodge that pure necessity was the motive of his absence.

REMARKS.

It is heartly to be wished that the knowledge of Geometry and Architecture, together with the rest of the sciences were the only entertainment of our modern Lodges: If so, what is often unhappily substituted in their places would not prevail as it does, neither ought a man to attain to any dignity in Masonry, without first having a competent knowledge in the liberal arts, and I am sorry to say that so few of that stamp are to be met with in the Lodges of this great metropolis, which defect is certainly owing (as heretofore observed) to the imprudent choice and introduction of their members, for every man formerly (tho' perhaps of a good and moral reputation) was not admitted into the Craft, nor allowed to share the benefits of our noble institution, unless he was endued with such skill in Masonry as he might thereby be able to improve the art either by plan or workmanship, or had such an affluence of fortune as should enable him to employ, honour, and protect the Crafstmen. I would not be understood by this to mean that no citizen or reputable tradesmen should receive any of our benefits; but on the contrary, am of opinion that they are valuable members of the commonwealth and in consequence would prove real ornaments to our Lodges; but how ridiculous is it to see daily so many persons of low life introduced amongst us (some of whom can neither read or write) and when they are admitted into the company of their betters by the assistance of Masonry, they too often act beyond their capacities, and (if the expression may be allowed) soon turn Mason mad, and under pretence of searching for knowledge, they fall into scenes of gluttonny or drunkeness, and thereby neglect their necessary occupations, and injure their families, which is not consistent with the known laws, constitutions, and principles of all true Brethren.

The by-laws and general regulations of the Lodges in this city are exceedingly well calculated for the good management of the Craft, but what avails the best contrived and most salutary laws if they are not put into form, and properly executed? To pass over indiscretions is in some measure granting a sanction or approbation of them, wherefore it highly concerns our worthy Masters to let no crime remain unremarked, but duly to admonish the offender, and if he repeats his transgression, to inflict such punishments as they and the Brethren shall judge necessary.

As my intention in taking notice of these transactions, is rather to reform than offend, I hope the guilty will answer my expectation, in laying aside these evil and too much frequented practices, and instead of affording blame for my advice, will attribute it to the real cause, *viz.* the overflovings of my respect, love, and sincere friendship for the Craft. Tis an indisputable maxim that authority and power ever produces awe and reverence, and consequently order and regularity amongst dependants.

REMARKS.

Altho' I am well ascertain'd that our principle commanders have always been noble, learned, and wise, yet of late years we have cause to mourn at our unhappy state, in sharing so little of their converse at our solemn meetings; nor can they blame us for our concern, since experience tells us, that when we often had the happiness of their presence, the Craft was enlivened, and nothing but joy and alacricy ran through the whole; and had it not been for the vigilance, care, and constant attendance of a most worthy grand officer (whose name I need not mention, since it is imprinted in indeliable characters on the breast of every true Brother in this city) the Grand Lodge would have felt almost an irreparable shock; but he, like a prudent governor, gained the hearts of his Brethren by cherishing their languispirits, and every one rejoyced in him,

If our noble Grand Master and his deputy would make a general visitation throughout the Lodges of this city (as hath been a custom according to the constitutions at least once in the year) the Brethren would be more careful in preserving that due harmony, and just decorum, which ought to shine amongst them, for as they would not be sensible of the hour of their Lords coming, they would always be upon the watch, and keep so strict a guard that irregularity or indiscretion would take no place amongst them, but on the contrary, the Craft would then appear in its pristine state, adorned with true and lasting glory, and its virtues conspicuously appear to all mankind. Having now described the cause of the present decay of Free-Masonry, together with some remarks, which I hope will be found useful to the Brethren shall give them the following friendly admonition, and then conclude.

As the Craft hath subsisted from times immemorial, and contains the most glorious precepts, of morality and virtue, let not the malicious world have cause to blame us for any base or degenerate actions, but let us industriously pursue the unerring rules which the Almighty Architect hath given us, let us all be united in one sacred bond of love and friendship, and if there is contention amongst us, let it be in striving who can out do each other in acts of religion, mercy, charity and all other good offices.

Let us all endeavour to deserve the following true character.

> If all the social virtues of the mind,
> If an extensive love to all mankind,
> If hospitable welcome to a guest,
> And speedy charity to the distressed,
> If due regard to liberty and laws,
> Zeal for our King, and for our country's cause,
> If these are principles deserving fame,
> Let Masons then enjoy the praise they claim;
> For
> Happy the innocent whose harmless thoughts,
> Are free from anguish as they are from faults.

F I N I S.

INTRODUCTION AND COMMENTARY TO

An Answer to the Pope's Bull, 1738
and
An Impartial Answer to the Enemies of Freemasonry, 1741

BY

Bro. R. E. PARKINSON, B.Sc., P.G.D. (I.C.)

SO little is known of the early history of the Grand Lodge of Ireland, owing to the loss of all official records before about 1760 and of Minutes before 1780, that any early references are worth investigation. The recent discovery [1] of a hitherto unknown, anonymous *Answer to the Pope's Bull*, published in 1738, and the long-lost *Impartial Answer to the Enemies of Free-Masonry*, by D'Assigny, published in 1741, are worth bringing to the notice of the Fraternity.

These two pamphlets are contained in a volume of miscellaneous pamphlets in the Library of Queen's University of Belfast, which include *An Appeal for a Legislative Union between England and Ireland*, dated 1704, *Barrack Regulations for Ireland*, sermons, and so forth; the only connecting thread seems to be that they are all concerned with Ireland and, with very few exceptions, published in that country. Inside the back cover is a Book Plate of the Campbell Arms, with the name "T. Campbell, A. B. 1756".

Thomas Campbell was the eldest son of the Rev. Moses Campbell, of Killeshil; born at Glack, Co. Tyrone, 4th May, 1733; entered Trinity College, Dublin, 15th April, 1752. Scholar, 1754, B.A. 1756, M.A. 1761, LL.B. and LL.D. 1772. Ordained Deacon, 31st May, 1761; Priest, 4th September, 1763. Curate of Clogher, 1761-72; Prebendary of Tyholland, 1772-3; collated Chancellor of Clogher, 8th February, 1773. He died in London, 20th January, 1795.

---

[1] By Bro. R. E. Parkinson, in May, 1964.

He was a well-known writer on miscellaneous subjects, and author of:

1. *A Philosophical Survey of the South of Ireland*; 8vo. Dublin, 1778.
2. *Strictures on the Ecclesiastical and Literary History of Ireland*; 8vo. Dublin, 1789, London, 1790.
3. *A Sketch of the Constitution and Government of Ireland down to 1783.*
4. *A Diary of a Visit to England in 1771-2.* Printed in Sydney, N.S.W., 1854, and *Johnsoniana*, Bohn's Series. It included a record of a visit to Dr. Johnson, mentioned by Boswell.
5. *A Sermon* preached at St. Andrew's, Dublin, 1780.

William Campbell, younger brother of Thomas, was Vicar of Newry, 1783-1804, and the volume bears the signature of his grand-nephew, the Rev. John Campbell Quinn, Curate of Donaghmore, near Newry, 1842-57, and Rural Dean of Aghaderg.

Among the subscribers to Spratt's *Constitutions*, 1744, were William Campbell and Patrick Campbell, and to Spratt, 1750, Richard Campbell, of Derry, and Andrew Campbell, of Newry. None of these, however, can I link with the clerical brothers.

Just when Speculative Freemasonry came to Ireland, it will, perhaps, never be possible to say. When the Dublin Guild of Carpenters, Millers, Masons and Heliers was incorporated by Henry VII in 1508, the Charter was granted to Walter, Archbishop of Dublin, Primate of Ireland, Gerald, Earl of Kildare, the Lord Deputy, several ecclesiastical dignitaries, judges, nobles and gentry, as well as operative craftsmen. It is tempting to assume that evolution followed much the same course as in England, stimulated, no doubt, from time to time by the constant coming and going across the Irish Sea.

At any rate, as the eighteenth century dawned, the time was ripe; Ireland, like England and Scotland, had suffered a century-and-a-half of civil and religious strife, and Lodges soon became meeting places for all men of goodwill, where political and religious differences were ignored.

The Established Church tended towards Latitudinarianism; the Bishops were largely English, and political appointments at that, forming a solid block in the House of Lords in the English interest. The Protestant Dissenters were mainly the Presbyterians of the north, whose ministers were largely trained at the University of Glasgow, where they came under the influence of Francis Hutcheson, himself a County Down man. Hence arose an increasing refusal to subscribe to the Westminster Confession of Faith, giving rise to a schism whereby the nonsubscribers were set apart in the Presbytery of Antrim. Deism was to be found—John Toland was a Derry man—but never obtained much acceptance, except by the advanced intelligentsia.

True, the Presbyterians suffered for their non-conformity and were debarred from public office, and there was a severe—even savage—code of laws on the Statute Book "To prevent the further Growth of Popery". Of this Irish Penal Code, two things must be said: first, it was no more severe than the laws in other countries of Europe restraining those who refused to conform to the State religion, and, secondly, it was rarely systematically enforced. It was rather kept as a rod in pickle to curb the "Papists" in time of stress. Nevertheless, there was a real spirit of toleration abroad. Conventions of the Religious Orders of the Roman Church were held from time to time in the city of Dublin itself, which could only have taken place with the connivance of government. The choral music of some of the Dublin Catholic Churches was of such a high order as to attract music lovers of all creeds.

Henry Barnewall, 4th Viscount Barnewall, was Grand Master of Ireland in the years 1733 and 1734. He was the head of an old Anglo-Norman Catholic family of the Pale and succeeded to the title in 1725. On 31st March, 1740, he presented himself at the House of Lords and took the Oath of Allegiance. He refused, on conscientious grounds, to subscribe to the declaration according to the English Act, and therefore never took his seat.

Presbyterians, mainly in the north, flourished, building their own meeting houses and adding to their congregations, governing themselves under the Presbyterian system with little interference.

Of course, extremists on all sides waged a wordy warfare; a scurrilous pamphlet published in Belfast, *True Blue Presbyterian Loyalty*, was speedily answered by the equally scurrilous *Jet Black Prelatic Calumny*.

Dublin was then expanding rapidly, to become the second city of the empire, and among the first half-dozen in Europe, in wealth and importance. The Mansion House was built in 1702 and the new Houses of Parliament opened in 1733. New streets and squares were rapidly laid out and adorned by the town houses of the nobility and gentry. The presence of 300 members of the House of Commons and a large number of peers and bishops led to a highly sophisticated social life.

The University was thriving; George Baldwin was Provost of Trinity College, the first for whom that office was not the stepping stone to ecclesiastical preferment. The great Library was built, with its "longest room in Europe". Swift lapsed into silence for some years before his death in 1745, and Berkeley was dwelling quietly in his Diocese of Cloyne, but continued to publish until shortly before his death in 1753. Burke and Goldsmith were at College in the 1740s, and many lesser lights kept the torch of literature and learning brightly alight. The theatre was flourishing, and everybody knows that Handel's "Messiah" was first performed in Dublin.

The social conscience was awakening; up and down the country, landlords were building almshouses for their aged tenants and schools for orphan children. Just as in London, where there was a wave of hospital building by private charity—Westminster, 1719, Guy's, 1725, St. George's 1733, the London, 1740, and Middlesex, 1745—in Dublin we have Cook Street Surgical, 1718; Dr. Steeven's, founded by a bequest of £600 per annum in 1710, was built between 1729 and 1733, Mercer's, 1734, and the Royal Hospitals for Incurables in 1744. The Cook Street Hospital was founded by six surgeons, among them Peter Brenan, whose brother, James, was Senior Grand Warden, 1732 and 1733, and Deputy Grand Master, 1734-1737. In the city of Cork, the South Charitable Infirmary was incorporated in 1722.

In 1737, some of the disabilities of the Irish Catholics were removed, and a further step towards emancipation was taken in 1777.

The Bull, *In eminenti*,[1] was formally published in Rome on 28th April, 1738. It is not quite clear why such a formidable weapon should have been launched against our Order, but it must be re-

---

[1] Chetwode Crawley, "The Old Charges and the Papal Bulls," *A.C.Q.*, xxiv, 1911, pp. 47-65, etc.

membered that, for the greater part of a century, England had been in the throes of revolution. One king had been beheaded and his family exiled; a parliamentary republic set up, to be followed by a military dictatorship, complete with "gauleites"; the monarchy restored, and a generation later the king exiled, his legitimate heir disinherited; first a Dutchman and later a German were called to the throne, both under terms dictated by Parliament. Little wonder, then, that English institutions were regarded askance by the conservatively minded, and that the appearance of Freemasonry on the Continent of Europe was greeted by the hostility of the governing powers in Holland in 1735, Sweden in 1736, and Paris, 1737.

The Roman Catholic Church has always claimed the right to control the lives of its adherents, not only in purely religious matters, but also in education, associations and even politics, especially in the days of temporal power.

Under William III, England had entered upon a war with France, which was not to end, in effect, till Waterloo, a century-and-a-quarter later. The suggestion [1] that the Pope felt that the establishment of Masonic Lodges throughout Europe was a subtle attempt by Walpole and the upholders of the Protestant Succession in England to provide foci of political influence is certainly plausible. The Old Pretender was in exile in Rome at the time, and the hope that a restoration of the Stuarts would bring back these islands into the fold of the Church was still very much alive. Many Irish and Scottish exiles had risen to prominence in the armies of France, Spain and Austria.

The Pope set forth his official objections in the Bull. Firstly, the association of men of different sects suggested, at best, an indifference to religious matters; at worst, an attempt to spread Deism or downright Atheism. The Order was governed by Laws and Statutes framed by itself, and the famous "Secret" was safeguarded by stringent oaths, taken upon the Sacred Book and reinforced by the most horrible penalties. This inviolable secrecy suggested that the work of the Lodges was of such an evil nature that they were forced to shun the light of publicity.

Any son of the Church defying the Bull would, *ipso facto*, incur excommunication, without any declaration. Absolution could be

---

[1] Alec Mellor, *Our Separated Brethren, the Freemasons*. Harrap, 1964.

granted by the Pope only, except on the point of death. Bishops were to take action, invoking, if need be, the aid of the secular arm and all that that implied.

A Bull is not binding on a Roman Catholic until it has been canonically published in his diocese and parish. The Bulls against Freemasonry were not so published in Ireland until 1799, after the Insurection of 1798, and then slowly throughout the country. They did not, indeed, become finally effective till half-a-century later, under the Primacy of Cardinal Cullen. Nor could they be fully effective without the aid of the secular power, which was not always forthcoming, even in Catholic countries, notably France.

I have been unable to date the anonymous *Answer to the Pope's Bull* more closely than the year given on the frontispiece, 1738—which in those days extended to the 25th March following. Nor can I suggest the author; it is manifestly inferior to D'Assigny's work, and was probably rushed out as soon as the news of the Bull reached Dublin. It is a mere denial of the charges. The device on the frontispiece is clearly not the product of a herald, but may merely be a representation of the White Horse of Hanover and a symbol of loyalty to the regime. The author descends to the sneer that, had the Pope been able to draw a revenue from the Lodges, they would have enjoyed his blessing.

But he also denies a charge not contained in the Bull, that of necromancy and devil worship. Lord Rosse, our first recorded Grand Master, is reputed to have founded and presided over the Dublin Hell Fire Club the previous year, 1737. It is doubtful, of course, whether this was more than a cover for orgies of hard drinking, gambling and wenching, rather than a serious form of Satanism!

Ireland, on the whole, seems to have been tolerably free from the waves of witch-hunting which swept over England and Scotland in the seventeenth and early eighteenth centuries,[2] though cases did occur. At Carrickfergus Assizes, on 31st March, 1711, seven old women of Islandmagee, Co. Antrim, were accused of bewitching a young girl, and were condemned to twelve months' imprisonment and to stand in the pillory four times during that period. The last instance was at late as 1808, again at Carrickfergus Assizes;

---

[2] St. J. D. Seymour, *Irish Witchcraft and Demonology*.

a woman was indicted for practising spells on a cow whose milk would not yield butter, and three victims died of suffocation from the fumes caused by the mixtures burned to relieve the spell. The accused was released by proclamation.

The only Irish Act against witchcraft was one of 1586; it seems to be doubtful if it was ever repealed. As late as 1913 an Irish Justice of the Peace was empowered to take cognizance of, among other crimes, "Witchcraft, Inchantment, Sorcery and Magic Arts". The last condemnation in England was in 1711, when a woman was condemned to death, and in 1722 in Scotland, when women were condemned to be strangled and burnt. The author's "Character of a Freemason" is based on the Old Charges; he denies the charge of Atheism or Deism, but his assertion that a Mason should strictly pursue the Religion of Nature would tend to encourage religious zealots in their opposition to the Order.

Our knowledge of Fifield D'Assigny still rests almost entirely on the research of Chetwode Crawley.[1] He was the grandson of one Pierre D'Assigny, said to have been a Walloon monk, who appears in London in 1636 as a convert to the Protestant faith. In 1638 he obtained the Rectory of St. Helier's, but five years later he turns up in Norwich, where he set up strife in the Walloon Church there. Six years later he returned to Jersey and, on the Restoration in 1660, disappears from view, leaving behind the unsavoury reputation of an unprincipled schemer.

By his second wife, whose name is unknown, Pierre was the father of Samuel, who became a notorious figure in Dublin towards the end of the seventeenth century, clad in clerical garb and discharging clerical functions, though there is the gravest doubt as to his regular ordination. In 1698 he published a violent Calvinistic polemic, and twelve years later an equally violent diatribe against the validity of Orders in the Roman Church. He apparently failed to obtain preferment in the Established Church, and took up the occupation of "Couple-beggar", or celebrant of unlicensed marriages.

His son, Fifield, was born in 1707. The forename is unusual, but a family of that name has been traced in the parish of St. Bride's, Dublin, at the time. The imposing array of letters after his name on

---

[1] Chetwode Crawley, *Caementaria Hibernica*, Fasc. II.

the title page of the *Impartial Answer* is rather difficult to interpret. Chetwode Crawley was satisfied that his name did not appear among the graduates of any University in these islands, nor in the lists of any of the licensing bodies. Nor does his name occur as a student at the University of Leyden, the most likely for a Huguenot to have studied on the Continent. Our chief authority on the hisory of medicine in Ireland suggests that the letters "A.S.L.L.S." may mean Apothecary Society Licentiate, and Licentiate in Surgery. It was just about 1740 that the apothecaries separated themselves from the mediaeval Guild of Barber Surgeons, Apothecaries and Peruke Makers to form their own Guild of St. Luke. Fifield D'Assigny died on Thursday, 10th January, 1744-5, and was buried in the churchyard of St. Werburgh's on the Sunday following. His funeral, as reported in the Dublin papers, was quite an elaborate affair, largely attended by his Masonic brethren, "properly cloathed", and by six Sergeants of the Foot, in their Regimentals and proper clothing.[2] This has led to the suggestion that D'Assigny may have held some appointment on the medical staff of the Army, but a search at the War Office, instigated by my good friend Bro. G. Norman Knight, has failed to trace his name.

The *Impartial Answer* is a work of some merit. The quotations from Virgil, Horace and other Latin authors, as well as references to various learned works, suggest that he had attained a fair standard of education. There is no hint of a knowledge of Greek, but his Latin reading would suggest that of the standard laid down for admission to the University of Dublin in those days.

The essay was read in the Grand Lodge of Ireland on 1st April, 1741, and was published with the approbation of that body. The concluding words of the dedication suggest that the Order of that day had still a strong Christian element. This is only to be expected, not merely from the essentially conservative attitude, which is still a tradition of the Irish Craft, but also on account of the very small numbers of the population who did not profess and call themselves Christian. From Cromwellian times there had always been a few members of the Jewish faith in Dublin and Cork, bringing their

---

[2] According to List of Dublin Lodges in D'Assigny-Spratt, Lodge 86 sat at Barrack Street. Lodge 86 in Col. Erwin's, later 5th Foot; but there is no mention of D'Assigny in the records of this Regiment.

gifts to the artistic and commercial life of the community, but at times their numbers fell below the minimum of ten heads of families required to establish a legal congregation.

D'Assigny lauds the fidelity of the brotherhood in maintaining the "Secret", and denies the charges of the profane that it must be preserved by the imposition of "some horrible and dreadful Oath". He goes on to point out that all civilized communities have found it necessary to impose oaths of various kinds for the protection of the public and the due performance of civic duties, and makes the remarkable statement that "oaths in our ART are not necessary, since Truth and Honour are the Principles by which we act".

He admits that there may be some unworthy members, but protests against the condemnation of the whole body for the faults of a few.

Published with the *Enquiry*, and with continuous pagination, is "The General Regulations of the Free and Accepted Masons of Ireland", based on Anderson, 1738, and "Approved of and agreed upon by the GRAND LODGE in DUBLIN, on the 24th of June 1741", so it is not unreasonable to assume that the *Enquiry* had at least semi-official approval. This ends with a List of the Regular Lodges in the city of Dublin, the last being No. 141, dated 6th February, 1743/4. This list contains sixteen Lodges, one of which, 86, was a Military one. Seven of the Lodges listed in Smith's *Pocket Companion*, published in Dublin in May, 1735, are omitted, and how many more (which may have been warranted between 1735 and 1743) had lapsed it is impossible now to say. From 1740 onwards the average number of Warrants granted yearly fell well below the number issued annually before that year. So that the decline was a very real one.

There had been some dispute—amounting to an incipient schism—over the election of a Grand Master in 1740. *Faulkner's Dublin Journal* of 1st July, 1740, has two distinct paragraphs, one recording the installation of the 3rd Viscount Doneraile at their ancient Hall in Smock Alley, and the other that of the Earl of Anglesey at the Roase Tavern, in Castle Street, on the same day, 24th June.[1] The causes of the dispute are somewhat obscure; Anglesey seems to have had the support of the more aristocratic element, but he

---

[1] Lepper & Crossle, *Hist. of the Grand Lodge of Ireland*, vol. i, p. 226.

was a thoroughly unsavoury character, excommunicated at the suit of his wife in 1741 for cruelty and adultery, and he was defendant in the notorious Annesley lawsuit of November, 1743, on the return from America of the true heir to the title, whom he was suspected of having got rid of.

The concluding words of the Preface to the *Enquiry* again bear witness to the strong element of Christianity in the Irish Craft—that the Brethren, "this life ended, may receive the recompense of their toils, and dwell in the presence of that immortal stone belonging to our building, even the Alpha and Omega of our redemption".

D'Assigny begins by a so-called "History" of Freemasonry from the time of Adam himself, and, referring to the Magi and Chaldees of Assyria, makes the significant comment: "But of these premises the Craft will receive a clearer information in a formed Lodge." He mentions the Kings of Scotland as patrons of the Royal Art, but unlike Pennell, has nothing to say about the ancient buildings of Ireland.

As to the decay of the Order, he ascribes this, firstly, to the lack of care in scrutinizing the qualifications of candidates for admission to the Order. He goes on to say that, some years previously, he had proposed in Grand Lodge that one month should elapse from the date of the proposal, during which two members should be appointed to investigate the qualifications of the candidate. He regretted that Grand Lodge did not approve his proposal, but it was to do so in the years to come. Regulation XIII of 1768 lays down that any Lodge in the City of Dublin having a man or men to be made shall give the Grand Secretary four days' clear notice in order that the Grand Officers and Inspecting Committee should be able to make any necessary enquiries. It is probable that these Regulations of 1768 comprised rules brought into force from time to time.[2]

Secondly, he suggests that the revival of the custom of visitation

---

[2] Nowadays, the qualifications of candidates are carefully scrutinized after the ballot, in Dublin by the Metropolitan Committee of Inspection, and in the Provinces by similar local Committees, each comprising one representative of each Lodge in the district. Moreover, it is normal for individual Lodges to appoint a Committee of two to report before the ballot, and in all cases the approach is a positive one. That is, it is the duty of the Committee not so much to ascertain that there are no objections, but rather to advance positive reasons why the applicant should be admitted.

of Lodges by the Grand Officers would ensure the preservation of that "due harmony and just decorum, which ought to shine amongst them". Again, Regulation XIV of 1768 provided that the several Lodges of the City of Dublin should be visited by a Select Committee of five or more members appointed by the Grand Lodge, provided that the Grand Master, his Deputy, the Grand Wardens, Grand Treasurer and Grand Secretary decline the same. The Committee, or any two of them, were empowered to inspect the books, the "Character and Conversations" of the members thereof, to ascertain if they had been duly registered and if they were clear of all dues.[3]

A third cause for the "Decay", D'Assigny suggests, was the multiplication of Degrees. The first use of the words "Royal Arch" in print occurs in *Faulkner's Dublin Journal* of 10th-14th January, 1743/4, describing a procession of Freemasons in Youghal, County Cork, on the previous St. John's Day: "Fourthly. The Royal Arch carried by two excellent Masons." Now, this may not mean any more than that a piece of apparatus known as the "Royal Arch" was borne in the procession; perhaps something of the nature of a Tracing Board, or even one of the wooden "Royal Arches" which still survive in some of our older Lodges: indeed, in some cases, these are still used in our older Royal Arch Chapters. The epithet "excellent" may have only have been added by the Secretary to lend colour to his report. At any rate, for what it is worth, there is no mention of the Royal Arch Degree in the surviving records of the Lodge concerned till about fifteen years later.

To his reference to Prince Edwin in his "history", D'Assigny adds as a footnote:—

"I am informed in that city [York] is held an assembly of Master Masons under the title of Royal Arch Masons, who as their

---

[3] With the vastly increased numbers of Lodges today, the Metropolitan Board of General Purposes discharges a similar function. In the Provinces, each Provincial Grand Master is entitled to appoint a number of Provincial Grand Inspectors, to each of whom a number of Lodges is allocated. It is their duty to visit the Lodges under their care from time to time, to assist them in any difficulties which may arise. They have power to inspect the books, and, in cases of indiscipline, to conduct a preliminary enquiry and report to the Provincial Grand Master. In Provinces overseas, Provincial Grand Inspectors are, in effect, Assistant Deputy Provincial Grand Masters.

qualifications and excellencies are superior to others they receive a larger pay than working Masons; but of this more hereafter."

Later, he protests that, although the land-marks of the constitution of Freemasonry are universally the same throughout all kingdoms, some had been led away by an impostor who posed as being a Master of the Royal Arch, which he had received in the city of York, but who had been exposed by one who had a short time before attained that "excellent part of Masonry in London". He goes on to refer to a certain itinerant Mason lately arrived in Dublin, whose eyesight was so strong as to bear the rays of the sun at noonday, and who professed to add three more steps to the three which the Dublin brethren had contented themselves to approach "our *Summum Bonum*, the immortal God". Thus it seems clear that, under the Grand Lodge of Ireland, a system of three Degrees was practised in Dublin, though his remark about the "*Summum Bonum*" would seem to imply that much more was contained in those three than in our present Craft system. Of course, they must have contained the substance of our present system, or else Dermott could not have proved himself to the brethren in London, but he always insisted that a "Modern" Mason could not be admitted to an "Antient" Lodge, as he had not been fully instructed. Could this possibly be the origin of the assertion that the Royal Arch Degree was formed by a mutilation of the old Third Degree?

The rival experts from York and Dublin suggest that two versions of the Royal Arch Degree were being promulgated in Dublin at the time, and it is worth remarking that two Legends were in use in Ireland down till 1864, when our persent ritual, based on the *repair* of the Temple under King Josiah was finally adopted. The other, more usual Legend, of the *rebuilding* under Zerubbabel, was also practised, some Chapters adhering to the one and some to the other. The Josiah legend has the merits of being based on a record in Holy Writ, and avoiding the anachronisms that disfigure the Zerubbabel version. It may also be of considerable antiquity; compare the oration delivered to the Grand Lodge of All England at York in 1726. There is also the interesting discovery of frescoes in Carpenters' Hall, London, in 1914.[1] The six degrees of the itinerant

---

[1] F. J. W. Crowe, "The Free Carpenters," *A.Q.C.*, 1914, xxvii.

Mason suggest French influence, and Dublin always had close links with France. The old Loge Anglaise at Bordeaux had many members in its earlier period with Irish names which can be identified. The Irishman has always been devoted to claret, while his English brother was content to imbibe the heavier beverages of Portugal. The butler of Trinity College still can boast that he and his predecessors have dealt with the same firm of wine merchants in Bordeaux for over 300 years!

Of the two recently-discovered pamphlets, the anonymous *Answer to the Pope's Bull* is quite trivial and little more than a curiosity, but D'Assigny's *Answer* contains a statement of principles as valid today as they were two centuries and a quarter ago. His *Enquiry*, of which a very brief review is included, apart from the light, however dim, it sheds upon the working of those days, presents solutions of problems in administration which may still arise.

AN ANSWER TO THE POPE'S BULL

and

AN IMPARTIAL ANSWER TO THE ENEMIES OF FREE-MASONRY

TWO RARE IRISH DOCUMENTS

by Fifield D'Assigny

AN ANSWER
TO THE
Pope's BULL;
WITH THE
Character of a Free Mason.
In an EPISTLE to the
Rt. Honourable and Rt. Worshipful Lord *MOUNTJOY*.
Grand MASTER of IRELAND.

Dublin : Printed and Sold by *Edward Waters* in *Dames'-street*, 1738.

Title-Page to *An Answer to the Pope's Bull*, Dublin, 1738

AN ANSWER

To the Pope's *BULL*, &c.

My LORD,

AS the Fraternity of F<small>REE</small> M<small>ASONS</small> have made such a Noise in the World, and have not only became dreadful to the Ignorant part of Mankind, but even suspicious to *some certain Powers*; I hope it will not be taken amiss, if I endeavour to paint their *Folly*, who blame that with which they cannot possibly be acquainted: And I must imagine, that it will appear as ridiculous in any of Them, as it wou'd in a Man, (altho' he had never been in *China*, and an entire Stranger to its Inhabitants, Laws, Constitutions, and Government;) who would confidently report, *That the People of that Nation were the most Disloyal, Rebellious, and wicked Subjects throughout the World*: And, that this is the Case with the *Enemies of Masonry* will plainly appear, when we consider of the insignificant Methods, with which They endeavour to persuade People against it; and because that they Themselves cannot arrive at the *Secret* in an illegal manner, are resolv'd to put others quite out of Humour with it, which they strive to do in the subsequent manner, by informing the World, *that* M<small>ASONS</small> *in their private Assemblies draw such Circles, and other strange Lines, that causes the Devil to pop up, and take his Place amongst Them*, which some say *is under the Table,* and others *as a Door-keeper.*

NOW, if the M<small>ASONS</small> are such *Conjurers* as to raise the Devil, and sit with calm and pleasant ease in his Company, I must boldly affirm, that I look upon Them to be Most Heroick, if not most Religious Men; for, as the Divines inform us, he is the general Enemy of Mankind, we cannot let him too much at defiance, and sure no greater can be, than that of face to face; but I cannot think it reasonable to believe that he is ever Employ'd as a *Door-keeper*, for as the Scripture describes him, to be so assiduous in grasping all that might come into his Reach, he would not be at all fit for that Office: But to be more serious, I suppose the World takes a distaste at MASONS, because they are true to their Words, and will not disclose the *least Secret* that is repos'd in their Breasts, altho' the breaking of the *One*, or the divulging of the *other*, seems to me an Argument of a most dishonest and treacherous Disposition: And I wou'd not have the World imagine, that they can ever arrive at the Perfection of the Art of *Masonry*, without first undergoing *a certain Operation*, which will entirely remove that Film that at present hangs over their visionary *Orb*; for, altho' they may be of Opinion that they see already very well, I durst venture to say, that they are as much in darkness at this time, as an unfortunate Prisoner, who is confin'd in such a Dungeon, that the least glimmering Ray of Light cannot possibly creep into him.

BUT among the many Enemies of *Masonry*, there hath lately started up a most formidable *One*, (and by some Reckon'd *Infallible*) I mean the *Pope*; who, as he tells us, judging that Fraternity highly to deserve *Ecclesiastical Censures*, hath issu'd out his *Bull of Excommunication*, which strictly forbids any *Catholick, to enter into, Countenance, or Defend Them*: His Holiness begins in the following Formal and Solemn Manner:

> IN the midst of the Cares of the Apostleship, and the continual Attention we have to extirpate *Heresies*, and maintain the Lord's Vineyard in its utmost Purity; We have heard with grief and bitterness of Soul, that a certain Society, who stile Themselves, *The Fraternity of* Free Masons, after making progress in several States in *Europe*, have likewise spread into *Italy*, and even there had some Increase. We have consider'd, that the Impenetrable Secret of this so Mysterious Society is the essential Part, and as it were the Basis of its Institution; and that being thereby become suspitious to the Temporal Powers, several of Them have proscribed it in their

Dominions. We have likewise consider'd, that by such stronger Reasons it ought to be suspitious to the Spiritual Power, whose Charge is to have an ever-watchful Eye over every Thing which may concern the Salvation of Souls. For these Reasons, and animated by our Pastoral Care, "we have Condemned, and do Condemn, by the present *Bull, &c. &c.*

THERE is no one that doubts but the Care of the Apostleship will ever be defended by His Holiness, or at least so long as there are Advantages attending it; but that he should stile the Society of FREE MASONS, or any other parcel of Men, by the Name of *Hereticks*, convinces me both of his Ignorance and Fallibility: And if the Truth was sufficiently known, *that grief and bitterness of Soul*, with which he seems so greatly to be oppress'd, does not proceed from any Spirit of Virtue animated by his *Pastoral Care*, or from an Opinion, that the Society of FREE MASONS commit Actions *either Base or Impure*, but rather from that part of his *Holiness's Wisdom*, which will not permit him to Approve of any, *but those who do Contribute towards the Increase of his Revenue and Treasures*: For, as he very prudently observes, *The Lord's Vineyard wou'd be in Danger of Starving*, or at least cou'd not be maintain'd in all its Purity without *those Benefices*; And I do not question, if the *Fraternity* wou'd allow him an *Annual Stipend*, to be disposed off according to the *charitable Discretion of his Holiness*, (which agreeable to an old Maxim, *often begins at Home*) but that he wou'd Approve of Them, nay, Condemn and brand with *Heresy*, all those who wou'd not come into the same way of thinking, and instead of declaring Them *suspitious to the Spiritual or Temporal Powers*, his Holiness wou'd insist on in the most strenuous manner, *That the Secret of Free Masonry was the very Basis of Religion, and so greatly conducing to the Welfare of Mankind, as to be even essential to the Salvation of their Souls.*

AND that this *Change* might be wrought in his Holiness will not seem improbable, when we take into our view the many *Brothel Houses* which are supported by his Protection in the Dominions of *Italy*; for which Favour a valuable Income yearly arises to him. Now in those Assemblies Vice generally appears in its various and most deformed Shapes, and I need not acquaint the Publick, that they have been ever found to debauch our Principles, as well as to destroy the peace and quiet of our Families, by dissolving Conjugal Love and Affection; Nay, they have been the cause of the greatest Evils which have happen'd to Mankind: These Iniquitous Practices his Holiness can pass over with an Eye of Approbation, without determining Them either pernicious to the Principles of State, or the Merit of Souls; but Those of the Fraternity of FREE MASONS (to which he is an absolute Stranger) cannot by any means be digested by him; wherefore his Holiness must excuse Us, if we believe that a *golden Key is sufficient to blind a* Pope, *and lock up all his Senses*; tho' God forbid that any of the *Fraternity* shou'd pay that Obedience to his *Supremacy, as to trample Reason under their Feet*; and methinks 'tis the Duty of every moral Man to shake off the Yoke of *Arbitrary Power* when leading to Destruction.

IF his Holiness and the Amazed Croud wou'd require to know, *what a strange and secret Man a* MASON *is*, I will describe him in the following manner.

THAT is, *One* who pays a due Reverence to his *Great Creator*, free from the *gross errors of Superstition*, or blind *Arrogance of Atheism and Deism*; *One* who is ever true and loyal to his Prince, dutiful and obedient to all higher Powers, provided they do not exceed the limited Bounds of Religion and Reason: *One* who is ever dispos'd to Contribute to the Welfare and Peace of his Country, utterly *abhorring any wicked Plots or dark Designs against the State*: *One* who never shuts his Ear unkindly to the Complaints of *wretched Poverty*, but with Patience hears, pitys, and relieves the *Distressed*: *One* who never gives the least Umbrage to Animosities and Contentions, but strives to promote a cordial Love and Friendship amongst the *Brethren*. In short, a MASON is *One* who strictly pursues the Religion of *Nature*, ever making that grand Precept of *doing unto others, as he would they should do unto him*; the main Center and Guide of all his Actions.

THESE are the Qualifications which every *true* MASON hath, and such as, in my Opinion, no Christian need to be asham'd to profess and Practise.

NOW, if his Holiness is not Content with this *Character* of a MASON, I wou'd advise him to send some of his Cardinals amongst them, who will perhaps return with the same Answer, as the Ministers of the Scotish Assembly did to their *Elders*, when dispatched on that Errand:

You may go yourself, and then you'll be satisfy'd.

I am, My Lord,

Your Most devoted humble Servant.

Philo-Lapidarius.

Frontispiece to D'Assigny's *An Impartial Answer to the Enemies of Free-Masonry.*

AN IMPARTIAL
ANSWER
TO THE
𝔈𝔫𝔢𝔪𝔦𝔢𝔰 of 𝔉𝔯𝔢𝔢=𝔐𝔞𝔰𝔬𝔫𝔯𝔶,

WHEREIN

Their unjust Suspicions, and idle Reproaches of that Honourable CRAFT, are briefly Rehearsed, and clearly Confuted.

To which are ADDED,

Several Serious Admonitions

Necessary to be observed

By that Antient FRATERNITY.

By *Fifield D'Assigny*, M. D. A. S. L. L. S.

———*Manet aliâ mente repôstum.*	Virg.
Quod de quoque Viro, & cui dicas sæpe Caveto.	Hor.

Publish'd by the Authority of the GRAND LODGE.

DUBLIN:
Printed by *Edward Waters* in *Dames'-street* and are to be Sold at his Shop, and at Mr. *Richard Pindar's* at the *White Hart* in *Pembroke-Court.*

Title-Page of D'Assigny's *Impartial Answer* . . .
Read in Grand Lodge on 1st April, 1741.

The Dedication.

TO THE

Free and *Accepted Masons*

Of the Kingdom of *Ireland*.

Well beloved Brethren,

HAVING *nothing more at Heart than the Welfare, Protection, and Advancement* of our Ancient and Honourable Craft; *and being truly sensible, that the Institution of our* Fraternity *was design'd for great and noble Uses, I have endeavour'd in the following Lines to Paint the Ignorance and Folly of such, who fond to show their Wit; Spleen, or Illnature, have attempted to render despicable the* most valuable Order *now on Earth.*

But notwithstanding the frequent Sallies of the undiscerning and malicious World, to accomplish that End, we have the Pleasure still to reflect, that with the greatest ease we have baffled and opposed their weak Designs, and smil'd in silence at their fruitless Labours; while our Royal and Noble Art, *like a well built* Fortification *hath stood secure against its cruel opposers, and yet remain'd impregnable, strongly resisting the most absolute Attacks of its viol'nt and daring Foes, who have not the Liberty to say, That 'twas ever in their Power, even once, to disappoint our mutual Intentions. For as our Work peculiarly consists in the Performance*

DEDICATION

of every Religious and Moral Virtue, in true and sincere Affection towards our worthy Labourers, who are join'd in the harmonious and united Bonds of such Fellowship, as proves to be the true and only Ornament of human Nature:

Why then should not we live on, like brave and honest Brethren, who strictly pursue those excellent and inimitable Rules, which our wise Forefathers have handed down to us, and who without either Fear or Trembling make it our chief Study to act pursuant to the glorious Pattern of that immortal Stone belonging to our Building, even the ALPHA & OMEGA of our Redemption.

I remain Brethren,

With cordial and unspotted Love; your

Fellow-Labourer in Good Works,

Fifield D'Assigny.

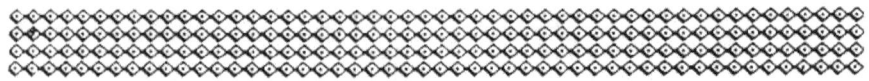

The Sanction.

THIS Piece was read by the AUTHOR to the GRAND LODGE, when assembled in due Form on the first Day of *April*, 1741, and was received with an universal APPROBATION.

John Baldwin, Esq; Secretary.

AN IMPARTIAL
ANSWER, &c

THE ART of FREE-MASONRY according to the most antient and authentick Histories, had its first Original above five thousand Years ago, which hath ever since been favour'd with a general Esteem from the Wise, Noble, and Learned of all Nations, who have not only Protected at all Times the MASTERS and FELLOW-CRAFTS of that wonderful Science, but have been pleased to condescend to lay aside their Regal and Princely Ornaments, nay to divest themselves of the glittering Trappings of State and Titles, and never thought themselves more happy and secure than when they wore the Indelible and Honourary BADGES of that ORDER.

By the help of this ART rude Nature was polish'd from her rustick Form, and the wild confus'd Particles of Matter were brought into Strength, Beauty and Proportion; while our great CREATOR, that All-Powerful MASTER MASON, hath shewn the Strength of his Wisdom and Knowledge, in the wide and beautiful Expanse of this lower World, which every where appears in the most minute PLANS of his CREATION.

And although it may be said, that many suspicious, Ignorant, and despotick POWERS have strove by barbarous and unreasonable Methods to force our Secret from us; yet have we with a fixt Resolution and undaunted Courage withstood the strongest Batteries of all their Threats and Temptations. Hunger and Thrift, the most powerful Calls of *Human Nature*, could never influence the stedfast and faithful BROTHER to impart his Soul to any of the *Pro-*

fane. And on the other Hand, when replete with *generous Liquor, that Opener of the Mind*, he hath still found a close Corner in his Breast to Repose this *Subject* with Safety: which hath also found means to escape the most artful Contrivances of *persuasive Women*, who in their soft Hours of Love, have frequently strove (tho' in vain) to wheedle out this *Matter* from such indulgent Men, as had no power of denying them any other Favour.

Then may we justly term Thee *thrice Honourable, thrice Mysterious* MASONRY, which hath preserv'd thy *Native Beauty*, and like a *Chast* [1] *Virgin*, who requires no other *Guard* but *Virtue*, hath always resisted the bold and rash Pursuits of each *intruding KNAVE*, and calmly despis'd the aspiring Attempts of the most *vigilant COWAN*.

Thou hast bound up in the confines of Privacy, the most froward Tongue, and taught the *Slanderer*, Silence: Thou hast restrained the Bents of the most lascivious Mind, and clip'd the Wings of loose Desire; and thereby prevented unlawful, and immodest Love.

Thou hast made the COWARD to discharge the mean Heart, that lurked within his Breast, and to assume that of Bravery and Resolution.

Thou hast untied the knotted Strings of *Avarice*, and caused the MISER, to discharge his much-lov'd *Store*, for *good* and *charitable Uses*.

Thou hast made the FOP to part his *Vanity, in admiring that dear Idol Himself*, and gladly to change his *gaudy Outside* for *better* and more lasting *Furniture within*.

Thou hast made *Man* to regard his CREATOR, with *a due Reverence*, and *religious Awe*, neither to suffer himself to be carried away with *blind Superstition*, or to be hurried on to follow the *arrogant Professors of ATHEISM* or *DEISM*.

And if it is objected, that MASONRY by its long continuance hath in some measure flowed in *muddy Streams*, where it may perhaps have contracted *Rust*; yet does the *Antique Fabrick* still remain, the *well-form'd Pillars* through the Rubbish apparently are seen: And though the *Superstructure* may be over-run with *Moss* and *Ivy*, the MODEL, now appears with the same additional

---

[1] *Sic.*

Splendour as the GLORIOUS SUN, when breaking from its dark and misty Clouds it comes to show itself at once the Comfort and Delight of Men. And I would only enquire of any Impartial Man of Reason, *Whether he would not justly prize the Venerable* BUST *of an antient* HERO, *who died for his Country's Cause, and whose Name, when living, was ever dear and memorable to the known Friends of Liberty; provided that valuable Representation had by some cruel Accident lost an Eye or a Nose.*

The Pride of the Antiquity of our ORDER, which we may justly boast off, was first formed when Distinctions among Men were not known, *Stars* and *Garters* were then but *Trifles*, for they had no other *Criterion* to jndge[1] of *Merit* by than a Man's *real Desert*, and he who took Care to *subdue his Passions, to lay a Curb on his unruly Appetites, and to observe the* GOLDEN RULE *of acting by others as he would they should do unto him,* (the main Centre and Guide of his Behaviour) was properly entitled to our *ORDER*; for these were the first Principles of *MASONRY*, which afterwards gave Encouragement to his followers to Invent, Study and Improve the liberal ARTS and SCIENCES, which the BRETHREN of all Countries have with indefatigable Industry, gave undeniable Proofs of their great and masterly Designs to all that part of the World, whom Ignorance and Obstinancy does not shade from the LIGHT. And methinks they deserve no pity, *who cast a Veil upon HEAVEN's first-born BLESSING*, and having Ears, resolve to be deaf to the Sounds of UNDERSTANDING: And that this is the Case with the ENEMIES of our *FRATERNITY*, will plainly appear, when the unprejudice'd Mind takes into view the many veteran and modern Edifices, compos'd with such Majesty and Art, as they in SILENT LANGUAGE sufficiently shew forth their Master's Praise, and in DUMB CHARACTERS demonstrate the Greatness of his SOUL.

And if the World will but consider us in our private Actions, they will soon discern (except a few mistaken Brothers) *That we are Friends to Virtue, and to its Friends, Alone; that we have Bowels of Compassion to pity the Fallen and Unfortunate, as well as Charity enough to hear their Complaints, and afford Succour to the Distressed.* And as these amiable Dispositions are inherent in every true MASON, I cannot imagine why the prying and uneasy

---
[1] *Sic.*

Multitude should give themselves such Concern about us, unless because they want a Knowledge or Power of Imitation; or that they perceive we shine with such superior Lustre, and excell them with its apparent Marks of Distinction, as they from the common Herd of the brutal Creation.

These are Motives, I confess, of Envy, and such as might be removed by an industrious and proper Application; But as Labour and Diligence is requisite for the Performance of any glorious Act, why should not they, before they reap the Fruits of our Vineyard, lend us an assisting Hand? No, forsooth, *they want to enjoy the Benefits without the Toil of Cultivating and Manuring it.* This prevailing Appetite is certainly contradictory to common Reason, Equity and Justice, and while those Creatures persist in that mode of thinking, nothing but *Darkness* must fall to their Share; for *GOLD*, that almost irresistable Argument cannot enforce us to accept of any but those, who after being try'd on the Touchstone of true Merit, have prov'd themselves the Standards of *Real Worth*.

Now where can be the Impiety of any Sett of Men congregating together, whose chief Aim and Intentions have always been form'd to *subdue their Passions, to promote their moral Qualities, and give Eucouragement to the most laudable ARTS*; and at the same time, *endeavouring to Improve, and to share with each other in the diverse Parts of necessary Skill, and usefull Knowledge*: So that the World must take a Pique at our *FRATERNITY*, for no other Reason *but because we do not like loquacious Bablers* disclose the Secrets that are repos'd in our Breasts; but when lodg'd there, keep them faithfully within the Limits of an honest Mind, and sooner than divulge the least Part thereof, which might betray our *Brother's Honour*, we have submitted to suffer even Rack and Torture. And for my part, I must ever be of Opinion, *That the keeping of a SECRET is the most distinguishing Characteristick of a generous and worthy Disposition, which from the Apprentice to the Privy Counsellor hath in all Ages been an Obligation highly to be regarded, and more especially since the contrary Method hath often been Productive of the greatest Evils among Mankind, nay, the Ruin of whole STATES and KINGDOMS have been occasioned by the want of a prudent TACITURNITY.* And as an excellent Proverbial Writer declares, *That the Words* of a Man's Mouth should be as deep Waters, and the Wellspring of Wisdom as a flowing Brook, for the Speeches of a Tale-Bearer give mortal Wounds, and affect the innermost and principle [1] Parts of the Body. Nor can the Sentence of honest *Plautus* enough be admired, who determined, *That those who could not bear the burden of Secrets, as well as those who were fond to hear them, should meet with the following Punishments, the Former to be hung up by their Tongues, the Latter by their Ears.* And because that we have so well preserv'd the Secrets of our Noble ART, they immediately conjecture and declare *that we are bound by some horrible and dreadful Oath,* to which I'll beg leave to Answer, *That in all civiliz'd Government it hath been a Custom* (for the better Preservation and Protection of their Rights and Priviledges) *to cause their Princes and Rulers to take certain Oaths, which example all wise Legislators have obliged their Officers, from the Highest to the Lowest, both in Church and State, to follow.* And no doubt it was contriv'd in order to restrain the turbulent Motions of Impious Consciences, and to rectify the base Appetites of some untoward Dispositions, insomuch that Tyranny, Injustice, and Oppression might be Strangers to their Breasts, whose Duty bound them to consult and act for the general Interest and Welfare of each Individual. Wherefore we plainly see, *that in all Undertakings, where the Good of Mankind was concern'd, an Oath was thought necessary for the better Performance thereof, which cannot be regarded in too solemn a manner*: And it is equally binding in matters of Trifles, as well as those of greater Importance, since Truth or Falshood [2] must appear in either. But OATHS in our ART are not necessary, since Truth and Honour are the Principles by which we act.

And I cannot see the Prejudice, *if* Thomas *takes an Oath to do Justice to his Neighbour* John, *to lend him such a Sum of Money, or Sell his Farm to him before any other Person*: So that the World are greatly mistaken when they imagine *that the Principles of MASONRY are weak or ridiculous,* for they are surely founded on the everlasting Basis of true RELIGION, moral and social VIRTUE.

The ANTIQUITY of our Noble ORDER descends in the Chain

---

[1] *Sic.*

[2] *Sic.*

of Time from the first Link of *ADAM*, on whose Heart the Almighty ARCHITECT engrav'd, even in his Sylvan LODGE, true Geometrical Proportion, and that amazing Symmetry that still remains among us: Nor shall our wise Grand Master *NOAH* be pass'd over in silence, who with a wonderful Contrivance, and divine Inspiration, erected a Wooden WORLD, to escape the fury of the mighty Waters, and thereby preserv'd the FAITHFUL from a general Deluge.

The Wise Men of *Ægypt* were also great Admirers of our SCIENCE, who under the Misterious Coverings of *Hieroglyphicks* hid their Secrets from the Vulgar and Uninitiated, and with profound Silence preserv'd their Benefits from all to whom they did not justly belong; nay so great a Veneration had they for Silence, that in their Temples they set up the Statute [1] of their God *HARPOCRATES*, who had his Right-hand plac'd near his Heart, and Cloathed with a Skin which before was full of Eyes and Ears, importing, *that many things may be heard and seen, but little Spoken.*

The Disciples likewise of old †*PYTHAGORAS*, were nearly attach'd to us, who follow'd their great Master in the pursuit of Symbolical Learning, and kept their Privacies without committing them to Writing, since by their Memory they were able to impart them to their Successors, as MISTERIES only fit for Gods.

And I cannot see what Reason our Enemies have to blame us for making use of particular SIGNS and WORDS, since they ever were the most distinctive Marks of the best and civil Societies; nay, amongst the Wisest Generals, *Are not watch Words given to their Soldiers, whereby the Friend from Foe may be distinguish'd?* This is the matter then of their Emulation against us, who are resolv'd to imitate such great Examples as in DARKNESS to receive the Benefits of LIGHT: For at the building of *Babel's* stupendous Tower, when Lips lost their usual Sound, and Languages in dark Confusion flow'd, our faithful BRETHREN made a solemn Engagement to communicate their sacred Mysteries (which were so highly recommended by the PATRIARCHS) to each other, that they might be handed down to all Posterity, and from this eternal Spring of Knowledge, thus receiv'd, we are able to distinguish the true

---

[1] *Sic.*

* Vide Imagines Deorum a vincentio Chartario.

† Vide Laertius de vita Pythagoræ.

Brother from the officious Eves-Dropper, or the busy Cowan, who knows not how to act upon the *SQUARE, that proper Emblem of divine Essence, where Beauty, Strength, and Harmony amazes our Eyes, and runs through the Whole, to make a finish'd Piece.

I cannot forebear mentioning the †Essenes amongst the *Jews*, who bore an Affinity to us, and did not disclose their *Misteries* to any until they had past certain degrees of Probation, and when the new Brother had covinced[1] the *SECT*, that he was Master of *Secrecy*, *Integrity*, and *good Manners*, they then conferr'd upon him further Knowledge, and properly inducted him into their most secret and valuable Priviledges; and then oblig'd him to live Uprightly, preserve his Faith and embrace the Truth, strictly to adhere to the Principles of Virtue, and above all things to avoid any Action which might bring an *Odium* or *Scandal* upon that *FRATERNITY*. So did the ‡*CABALISTS*, and Antient §*DRUIDS* amongst the *Britons*, as well as many other learned Societies of Men, too numerous to be inserted in the Compass of these Sheets, who all retain'd and preserv'd their Wisdom by Oral Tradition.

Thus much for Antiquity: Now must I beg leave to Inform our Enemies, *That we look on the Prosperity of no* Society *with Eyes of Envy or Malice, nor without Fear or Wit, rail at them as they at us, Unheard, Untry'd, but innocently Laugh at such gross Ignorance, and impotent Malice; while we with agreeable Converse, endeavour to give a relish to the nauseous Draughts of Life, and cause them to flow down with greater smoothness*: To State disputes we give no Birth, to Anger or Contentions, no Umbrage, to impure Discourse, no Ear, to idle and licentious Oaths, no Tongue, to Persecution, an absolute Hatred, and to Peace, as

---

* The *Pythagoreans* held that a Square was the proper Emblem of Divine Essence, for the gods, they say, who are the Authors of every thing establish'd in Wisdom, Strength and Beauty; are not improperly represented by that Figure.

† Vide Philo de vita Contemplativa.
  Josephus antiq; lib. 8 Cap. 2.

[1] *Sic.*

‡ Vide Basnages Hist. of the Jews on Cabala.

§ Vide Cæsar Com. lib. 6.
  Samms Hist. of Brit. Book 1 Chap. 4.

great a Love; thus with a due deference to our Superiors, we Spin the Threads of our Days in joyful HARMONY and just Proportion; and tho' upon the LEVEL with our BRETHREN, never beyond COMPASS, and within the Limits of the SQUARE and PLUMB.

As to the ridiculous Inventions of the Vulgar to asperse our FRATERNITY, I mean, *such as raising the Devil, Conversing with infernal Spirits, the wild Story of an old Woman between the rounds of a Ladder, the Cook's red hot Iron, or Salamander, with many more of the same idle Stamp*, I shall pass over with Compassion towards them, as beneath the Notice of Men of Reason, since they never had any Foundation for such Faith, but what proceeded from their dark Ignorance. To them our CRAFT shall ever stand as a PYRAMID of AMAZEMENT, as it hath hitherto done, with the Generous and Brave a lasting MONUMENT of GLORY: But those who argue with moderate humour, and would enquire into the Cause, *why some of our FRATERNITY are liable to the Failures of human Nature, and even tainted with some deform'd and vicious Appearances?* I Answer, *That in so great a number of Men it is not to be wonder'd at if here and there an* APOSTLE *turns an* APOSTATE. And as too many have the Art of cloaking their Vices under the colour of Sanctity, *How is it possible that a human Eye can discover the black Ideas of their Minds?* No, that Knowledge meets with an universal Blank, except from one to whom all Hearts are open and every Action known before 'tis brought into Motion: And how unequitable is it then to blame a whole Society for some few mistaken Men? whose unhappy Failures cannot affect or depreciate our glorious ART, still unspotted and undefiled, no more than true RELIGION can be defaced by wicked and blasphemous Professors. And tho' some iniquitous Wretches have labour'd to give a Stab to Both, yet we with the greatest Satisfaction view all their attempts prove as fruitless as if they strove to change the Complexion of the *Æthiopic*, or deprive the *Leopard* of his Spots: And Experience sadly convinces us, *That neither Scripture nor Reason will polish the evil Stamps of some preverse Minds*; wherefore with Pity we must Compassionate those unhappy Dispositions, and endeavour to preserve our Conscience void of Offence towards our great CREATOR and our BRETHREN.

Serious Admonitions, &c.

———— *Si quid Novisti rectius istis*
Candidus imperti, Si non, his utere mecum.   Hor.

YE Immortal *_NOACHIDÆ_, hear my Words, and let not the Truth forsake thee, but bind it about thy Necks with Hoops of Steel: Let not the malicious WORLD have cause to give ye blame, whose antient Customs have been admired from time immemorial, and I hope will still deserve the same esteem from the most eminent of Ages yet to come, and increase in Splendour while the Sun shoots from its radiant Beams, or the Moon its pale Nocturnal Reflection.

Preserve your antient LAWS and CHARGES, and let your Constitutions be the Guide of your Actions; but particularly observe to pay due and proper Homage to that most august and glorious Body, *The GRAND LODGE of this Kingdom*, which I hope will ever be adorned with such dazzling Patterns as our late GRAND MASTERS, and I should think myself somewhat remiss if I did not inform you of the assiduous and prudent Methods that our Grand Officers have lately taken to increase the Benefits of our Common-Wealth, wherefore let each Brother pay to them a decent Tribute of Praise, for their constant Attendance, their great and learned Counsells are sufficient Marks of the Elegance of their taste in Architecture, and of their sincere Warmth and Affection to our CRAFT, and of that true Spirit of *MASONRY* which they have so often shewn, and which will not only render them the Delight of our present BRETHREN, but the Admiration of all Future.

---
* The most ancient Word for *Masons* that can be found in their Records.

In your private Lodges be subservient to those wholesome By-laws, which have been made for your Uses, and are consistent with the old Rules of MASONRY, for each Deviation from them, will not appear in a good Light before our excellent MASTERS.

Be cautious to whom ye afford your Benefits, and let not Poverty or any other Motive influence any of you to sell your BIRTH-RIGHTS for a Mess of POTTAGE, but like true MASONS, and as ELECT amongst Men prove that you are the real thing you represent. Let no clandestine ACTS Eclipse your CHARACTERS, but like judicious POTTERS see that your CLAY is well temper'd, free from the least unseemly Blemish before you make your VESSEL, for such omission often destroys the Beauty of your WORK.

Let not excess of Liquor destroy your REASON or waste your SUBSTANCE; but behave both in Celibacy and a Matrimonial Life, in such a manner as may convince the unbelieving WORLD, that MASONRY hath not lost it's pristine Decorations. Let Slander and Envy be banish'd from your *Breasts*; despise not one Another, *for Detracting a Brother's Character is spoiling your Own, and giving the World the same opportunity of judging of yourself: 'Tis robbing him of his dearest Part, his Reputation, which does not enrich you, but makes him Poor indeed*. And, you shou'd consider, that the most doubtful *Accusations*, are always found from the general and prevailing Ill-Nature of Mankind, *to leave a Sting behind Them;* and as the Poet elegantly says,

> *On Eagles Wings pernicious Scandals fly,*
> *While virtuous Actions are but Born, and die!*

Men of this cruel way of Thinking, are a pest to Governments, and hurtful to all Societies; and, I think, they may be justly compared to the *Looking-Glasses* in the Temple of *Smyrna*, which represented the fairest and best featured Face, as a most deformed and frightful appearance; In short I wou'd advise you to Reflect, *That he who sells his Brother's Credit at a low price, perhaps, may make a Market for others to purchase his own at the same Rate.* Avoid then speaking Evil of him at any time, but defend his *Character* as far as is consistent with the safety of your own Honour.

Now remains a noble Virtue, which our great Limners in the Portraiture thereof, have Represented in the form of a *naked*

* Babe, having a sprightly Countenance, and surrounded with a Cloud; in its Right Hand holding a bloody Heart, in its Left, affording Honey to a Bee without Wings; which Draught seems to Import, that *Charity ought to be as humble as a Child, and all her Gifts bestowed with a Chearful Will.* The bleeding Heart must signify, *the pain a good Brother feels when he sees, and pitys the Distressed*: And that Honey which is given to the Bee without Wings, *is that Succour which should be afforded to the Unfortunate who cannot help Themselves.* Therefore fail not to aid, by your Advice, and supply with your Purse, *the Necessities of the Indigent Supplicant, for all your Treasure is but in Trust for him*; And, he who detains a Mite from his needy Brother, when in his power, without hurting himself, certainly commits an act of Injustice. Therefore, my Brethren, act as that learned Apostle St. *Paul* advises, *Put on Bowels of Mercy, Kindness, Humbleness of Mind, and above all these things put on Charity, which is the Bond of Perfectness*: And be not like that Miser, who, when on his death-Bed put as much Gold in his Mouth, as he could possibly contain therein; and being ask'd the reason for so doing, answered, *That some were wiser than others, and that he purposed to keep that safe until he was dead.*

Reject all PRETENDERS as Men of base and ignoble Principles, and take at all times an especial care that your House be well Tyled, and your Materials kept close in an Ivory Receptacle, while awful Silence with a Sword of Faith stands Guardian at the Door, and every *Brother* keeps his Key. And be not like the false † *Hipparchus* who was expell'd by *Pythagoras* for his infamous Dealings, and having lost all sense of Honour, the good Philosopher, as a punishment of his crime, ordered a Tomb to be made for him, while living; the reflection of the Shame of which, threw the Wretch into a violent fit of Madness, insomuch that he committed that monstrouse crime of Suicide, by cutting his own Throat: So was his Memory amongst *good Men* thus much abhorred, that after his death he lay upon the Island of *Samos*, where the Sands of the Sea were his deserved Sepulchre.

---

* This Emblem of Charity is Represented in the Copper-plate at the Frontispiece.

† Clem. Alexandr. Strom.

To Conclude, May the ROYAL ART go on and Prosper, spreading its Glories from Pole to Pole, while *Learning, Trade* and *Liberty* shall flourish; and may it be ever countenanc'd by the most eminent POTENTATES, since it hath always been a Favourite of the politest Kingdoms: Thus may it still continue, in spite of all that *Treachery, Ignorance,* or *Malice* can contrive to Overthrow it.

And may it Live 'till Nature fades away,
And gives a Groan, expressing its Decay.

FINIS.

THE

General REGULATIONS

Of the FREE and ACCEPTED

MASONS

IN THE

Kingdom of *IRELAND*,

Pursuant to

The *English* CONSTITUTIONS,

Approved of and agreed upon by the GRAND LODGE in *DUBLIN*, on the 24th of *June* 1741.
TULLAMORE Grand Master.

D U B L I N:
Printed by *Edward Bate* for the AUTHOR,
M,DCC,XLIV.

To the Rt. Worshipful and Rt. Honourable

The Lord Vifc. ALLEN,

Grand Master of Free and Accepted Masons in the Kingdom of IRELAND

My LORD,

AS nothing can be more conducive to the order and harmony necessary to our Society, than to be fully acquainted with the good and wholesome laws and charges which have by our learned predecessors and Brethren been curiously and ingeniously compiled for our better conduct in life; so nothing can give me more pleasure than to be commanded by (that August body) the Grand Lodge, to transcribe the following regulations and lay them before your Lordship.

The Grand Lodge in order to prevent any disputes or differences which may possibly arise among our younger Brethren, thro' the want of knowledge in our antient and well founded constitution, have prudently thought proper to direct the regulations to be published, and by that means, let every Brother know how he shall be able to conduct his actions with uprightness and integrity, and that morality and Brotherly love, with all the social virtues (the proper embellishments of the Fraternity) may be equally diffused thro' the whole.

When we call to mind the many attempts that have been made to subvert our most antient constitution (which hath subsisted from the earliest account of time), and the many ridiculous aspersions that the ignorant multitude (thro' prejudice only) have endeavoured to cast upon the worthy professors of our most antient and noble Craft, for their fidelity and circumspection therein they will I make no doubt be motives sufficient to prevail upon your Lordship to concur in publishing to the world our most excellent regulations; and thereby convince those who are prejudiced against our fraternity, that our constitution is founded on truth, justice, and, charity.

Our Brethren have the highest sense of your Lordship's affection for the Noble Craft, and cannot avoid promising themselves that under your influence they will be able to obviate any ill grounded censures, that the enemies of the fraternity may at any time pass upon them.

I am, my Lord, with due respect,

Your Lordship's

most humble,

most Obedient servant,

and faithful Brother,

EDWARD SPRAT.

The General REGULATIONS of the Free and Accepted Masons in the Kingdom of IRELAND, &c.

Old Regulations.

I. THE Grand Master or his Deputy has full authority and right, not only to be present, but also preside in every Lodge, with the Master of the Lodge on his left hand; and to order his Grand Wardens to attend him, who are not to act as Wardens of particular Lodges but in his presence and at his command: for the Grand Master, which in a particular Lodge may command the Wardens of that Lodge, or any other Master Masons, to act there as his Wardens *pro tempore.**

II. The Master of a particular Lodge has the right and authority of congregating the members of his Lodge into a chapter upon any emergency or occurrence; as well as to appoint the time and place of their usual forming: and in case of death or sickness, or necessary absence of the Master, the senior Warden shall act as Master *pro tempore*, if no Brother is present who has been Master of that Lodge before:

New Regulations.

I.* THAT is only when the Grand Wardens are absent: for the Grand Master cannot deprive them of their office, without shewing cause fairly appearing to the Grand Lodge according to the old regulation XVIII. so that if they are present in a particular Lodge with the Grand Master, they must act as Wardens there.

II. It is agreed that if a Master of a particular Lodge is deposed or demits, the senior Warden shall forthwith fill the Masters chair till the next time of chusing; and always in the Master's absence he fills the Chair even tho' a former Master be present.

Old Regulations.	New Regulations.

for the absent Masters authority reverts to the last Master present, tho' he cannot act till the senior Warden has congregated the Lodge.

III. The Master of each particular Lodge, or one of the wardens, or some other Brother by appointment of the Master, shall keep a book containing their by laws, the names of their members, and a list of all the Lodges in town; with the usual times and places of their forming: and also all the transactions of their own Lodge that are proper to be written.

III. If a particular Lodge remove to a new place for their stated meetings, the officers shall immediately signify the same to the secretary.

The precedency of Lodges is grounded on the seniority of their constitution.

IV. No Lodge shall make more than five new Brothers at one and the same time without an urgent necessity; nor any man under the age of twenty five years (who must also be his own master) unless by a dispensation from the Grand Master.

IV. It was agreed that no Brother should belong to more than one Lodge within the bills of mortality; but for several reasons it is now obsolete.

V. No man can be aceepted a member of a particular Lodge without previous notice one month before given to the Lodge; in order to make due enquiries into the reputation and capacity of the candidate, unless by a dispensation.

V. The secretary can direct the petitioner in the form of a dispensation, if wanted. But if they know the candidate they don't require a dispensation.

VI. But no man can be entred a Brother in any particular Lodge, or admitted a member thereof without the unanimous consent of all the members of that Lodge then present when the candidate is proposed, and

VI. No visitor, however skilled in Masonry, shall be admitted into a Lodge, unless he is personally known to, or well vouched and recommended by one of that Lodge then present. But it was found inconvenient

| Old Regulations. | New Regulations. |

when their consent is formally asked by the Master. They are to give their consent in their own prudent way, either virtually or in form, but with unanimity. Now is this inherent priviledge subect to a dispensation; because the members of a particular Lodge are the best judges of it; and because if a turbulent member should be imposed on them, it might spoil their harmony, or hinder the freedom of their communication, or even break and disperse the Lodge, which ought to be avoided by all true and faithful Brethren.

to insist upon unanimity in several cases: and therefore the Grand Masters have allowed the Lodges to admit a member, if not above three ballots are against him; though some Lodges desire no such allowance.

VII. Every new Brother, at his entry, is decently to cloth the Lodge, that is, all the Brethren present; and to deposite something for the relief of indigent and decayed Brethren, as the candidate shall think fit to bestow, over and above the small allowance that may be stated in the by-laws of that particular Lodge: altho' the candidate shall solemnly promise to submit to the constitutions and other good usages, that shall be intimated to him in time and place convenient.

VII. Only particular Lodges are not limited, but may take their own method for charity.

VIII. No set or number of Brethren shall withdraw or separate themselves from the Lodge in which they were made, or were afterwards admitted members, unless the Lodge become too numerous; nor even then

VIII. Every Brother concerned in making Masons clandestinly, shall not be allowed to visit any Lodge till he has made due submission, even tho' the Brothers so made, may be allowed. None who from a stated

| *Old Regulations.* | *New Regulations.* |

without a dispensation from the Grand Master or deputy: and when thus separated, they must either immediately joyn themselves to such other Lodges that they shall like best, or else obtain the Grand Masters warrant to joyn in forming a new Lodge to be regularly constituted in good time.

Lodge without the Grand Masters leave shall be admitted into regular Lodges till they make submission and obtain grace.

If any Brethren form a Lodge without leave, and shall irregularly make new Brothers, they shall not be admitted into any regular Lodge, no not as visitors, till they render a good reason and make due submission.

If any Lodge within the bills of mortality shall cease to meet regularly during twelve months successive, its name and place shall be erazed out of (or discontinued in) the Grand Lodge book: and if they petition to be again incerted and own'd as a regular Lodge, it must loose its former place and rank of precedency, and submit to a new constitution.

Seeing that some extraneous Brothers have been made lately in a clandestine manner, that is, in no regular Lodge nor by any authority or dispensation from the Grand Master, and upon small and unworthy considerations, to the dishonour of the Craft;

The Grand Lodge decreed that no person so made, nor any concerned in making him, shall be a Grand officer, nor an officer of a particular Lodge, nor shall any such partake of the General charity if they should come to want it.

| *Old Regulations.* | *New Regulations.* |

IX. But if any Brother so far misbehave himself as to render his Lodge uneasie, he shall be thrice duly admonished by the Master and Wardens in a Lodge formed: and if he will not refrain his imprudence, nor obediently submit to the advice of his Brethren, he shall be dealt with according to the by-laws of that particular Lodge, or else in such a manner as the quarterly communication shall in their great prudence think fit; for which a new regulation may be afterwards made.

IX. Whereas disputes have arisen about the removal of Lodges from one house to another and it has been questioned in whom that power is vested; it is hereby declared,

That no Lodge shall be moved without the Master's knowledge; that no motion be made for moving in the Master's absence; and that if the motion be seconded or thirded, the Master shall order summons to every individual member, specifying the business, and appointing a day for hearing and determining the affair, at least ten days before: and that the determination shall be made by the majority, provided the Master be one of that majority; but if he be of the minority against removing, the Lodge shall not be removed unless the majority consist of full two thirds of the members present.

But if the Master shall refuse to direct such summons, either of the Wardens may do it: and if the Master neglects to attend on the day fixed, the Warden may preside in determining the affair in the manner prescribed; but they shall not in the Masters absence, enter upon any other cause but what is particularly mentioned in the summons: and if the Lodge is thus regularly ordered to be removed, the Master or Warden shall send notice

Old Regulations.	New Regulations.
	thereof to the secretary of the Grand Lodge for publishing the same at the next quarterly communication.
X. The majority of every particular Lodge when congregated (not else) shall have the priviledge of giving instructions to their Master and Wardens before the meeting of the Grand chapter or quarterly communication; because the said officers are their representives, and are supposed to speak the sentiments of their Brethren at the said Grand Lodge.	X. Upon a sudden emergency the Grand Lodge has allowed a private Brother to be present, and with leave asked and given to signify his mind, if it was about what concern'd Masonry.
XI. All particular Lodges are to observe the same usage as much as possible; in order to which, and for cultivating a good understanding among Free-Masons, some members of every Lodge shall be deputed to visit the other Lodges as often as shall be thought convenient.	XI. The same usages, for substance, are actually observed in every Lodge; which is much owing to visiting Brothers who compare the usages.
XII. The Grand Lodge consists of, and is formed by, the Masters and Wardens of particular Lodges upon record, with the Grand Master at their head, the deputy on his left hand, and the Grand Wardens in their proper places,	XII. No new Lodge is owned, nor their officers admitted into the Grand Lodge, unless it be regularly constituted and registered.
These must have their quarterly communications and adjournments as occasion requires, in some convenient place, as the Grand Master shall appoint; where none are to be present but its own proper members,	All who have been or shall be Grand Masters, shall be members of and vote in all Grand Lodges.
All who have been or shall be Deputy Grand Masters shall be members of and vote in all Grand Lodges.
All who have been or shall be Grand Wardens shall be mem-

| *Old Regulations.* | *New Regulations.* |

without leave asked and given: and while such a stranger (tho' a Brother) stays, he is not allowed to vote nor even to speak to any question without leave of the Grand Lodge or unless he is desired to give his opinion.

XIII. At the Grand Lodge in quarterly communications, all matters that concern the fraternity in General, or particular Lodges, or single Brothers, are sedately and maturely to be discoursed of.

1

Apprentices must be admitted Fellow-Crafts and Masters only here, unless by a dispensation from the Grand Master.

2

Here also all differences that cannot be made up or accomodated privately, nor by a particular Lodge, are to be seriously considered and decided: and if any Brother thinks himself aggrieved by the decission, he may appeal to the annual Grand Lodge next ensuing and leave his appeal in writing with the Grand Master the Deputy or Grand Wardens.

3

Hitherto all the officers of

bers of and vote in all Grand Lodges.

Masters and Wardens of Lodges shall never attend the Grand Lodge without their jewels and clothing, except upon giving sufficient reasons.

If any officer cannot attend, he may send a Brother of that Lodge (who has been an officer before) with his jewel to supply his room and support the Honour of his Lodge.

XIII. What business cannot be transacted at one Lodge may be referred to the committee of charity, and by them reported to the next Grand Lodge.

The Master of a Lodge with his Warden and competent number of the Lodge assembled in due form, can make Masters and fellows at discretion.

It was agreed that no petitions and appeals shall be heard on annual Grand Lodge day, nor shall any business be transacted that tends to interrupt the harmony of the assembly, but shall be all referred to the next Grand Lodge.

Old Regulations. | *New Regulations.*

particular Lodges shall bring a list of such members as have been made or even admitted by them since the last Grand Lodge.

There shall be a book kept by the Grand Master or Deputy, or rather by some Brother appointed secretary of the Grand Lodge; wherein shall be recorded all the Lodges, with the usual time and places of their forming and the names of all the members of each Lodge: also all the affairs of the Grand Lodge that are proper to be written.

4

The Grand Lodge shall consider of the most prudent and effectual method of collecting and disposing of what money shall be lodged with them in charity, towards the relief only of any true Brothers fallen into poverty and decay, but of none else.

But each particular Lodge may dispose of their own charity for poor Brothers according to their own by-laws.

They shall also appoint a treasurer, a Brother of good worldly substance, who shall be a member of the Grand Lodge by virtue of his office, and shall be always present, and have a power to move to the Grand Lodge any thing that concerns his office.

To him shall be committed all

| Old Regulations. | New Regulations. |

mony raised for the general charity, or for any other use of the Grand Lodge; which he shall write down in a book with the respective ends and uses for which the several sums are intended, and shall expend or disburse the same as the Grand Lodge shall at any time agree upon.

5

But by virtue of his office as treasurer, without any other qualification, he shall not vote in chusing a new Grand Master and Wardens; tho' in every other transaction.

In like manner the secretary shall be a member of the Grand Lodge by virtue of his office, and shall vote in every thing except in chusing Grand officers.

The treasurer and secretary may each have a clerk or assistant, if they think fit, who must be a Brother and a Master Mason; but must never be a member of the Grand Lodge, nor speak without being allowed or commanded.

The Grand Master or Deputy have authority always to command the treasurer and secretary to attend him with their clerks and books; in order to see how matters go on and to know what is expedient to be done upon any emergency.

Another Brother and Master Mason should be appointed the

Old Regulations.

tyler, to look after the door; but he must be no member of the Grand Lodge.

XIV. If at any Grand Lodge stated or occasional quarterly or annual, the Grand Master and Deputy should both be absent; then the present Master of a Lodge shall take the Chair by the rule of rotation, and preside as Grand Master *pro tempore*, and shall be invested with all his honour and power for the time being; provided there is no Brother present that has been Grand Master or Deputy formerly; for the last former Grand Master or Deputy in company takes place of right, in the absence of the present Grand Master or Deputy.

XV. In the Grand Lodge none can act as wardens but the present Grand Wardens if in

New Regulations.

XIV. The right of Grand Wardens was omitted in this regulation; and it is has been since found that the old Lodges never put into the Chair the Master of a particular Lodge, but when there was no Grand Warden in company, present or former, and that in such a case a Grand officer always took place of any Master of a Lodge that has not been a Grand Officer.

Therefore in case of the absence of all Grand Masters and Deputies, the present senior Grand Warden fills the Chair, and in his absence, the present junior Grand Warden, and in his absence the oldest former Grand Warden in company, and if no former Grand officer be found, then the Master of a Lodge by the said rule of rotation.

But to avoid disputes, the Grand Master usually gives a particular commission under his hand and seal of office, counter signed by the secretary to the senior Grand Warden, or in his absence to the junior, to act as Deputy Grand Master when the Deputy is not in town.

XV. The Grand Lodge finding it was always the antient usage that the oldest former

Old Regulations.	New Regulations.
company; and if absent the Grand Master shall order private Wardens to act as Grand Wardens *pro tempore*; whose places are to be supplyed by two Fellow Crafts or Master Masons of the same Lodge, called forth to act or sent thither by the Master thereof; or if by him omitted, the Grand Master or he that presides shall call them forth to act, that so the Grand Lodge may be always compleat.	Grand Wardens supplied the places of those of the year when absent, the Grand Master ever since has ordered them to take place immediately and act as Grand Wardens *pro tempore*; which they have always done in the absence of the Grand Wardens for the year, except when they have waved their priviledges for that time, to honour some Brother whom they thought more fit for the present service.
	But if no former Grand Wardens are in company, the Grand Master or he that presides calls forth whom he pleases to act as Grand Wardens *pro tempore*.
XVI. The Grand Wardens, or any others, are first to advise with the Deputy about the affairs of the Lodges or of private single Brothers; and are not to apply to the Grand Master without the knowledge of the Deputy, unless he refuse his concurrence. 1	XVI. This was intended for the ease of the Grand Master, and for the honour of the Deputy. 1
In which case or in case of any difference of sentiments between the Deputy and Grand Wardens or other Brothers, both parties are to go to the Grand Master by consent; who by virtue of his great authority and power, can easily decide the controversy and make up the difference. 2	No such cases happened in our time and all Grand Masters governed more by love than power. 2
The Grand Master should not	No irregular applications have

| Old Regulations. | New Regulations. |

receive any private intimations of business concerning Masons and Masonry but from his deputy first, except in such cases as his worship can easily judge of: and if the application to the Grand Master be irregular, his worship can order the Grand Wardens, or any other so applying, to wait upon the Deputy, who is speedily to prepare the business and to lay it orderly before his worship. 3

been made to the Grand Master in our time. 3

XVII. No Grand Master, Deputy Grand Master, Grand Warden, treasurer, secretary, or who ever acts for them or in their stead *pro tempore*, can, at the same time, act as the Master or Warden of a particular Lodge; but as soon as any of them has discharged his publick office, he returns to that post or station in his particular Lodge from which he was called to officiate.

XVII. Old Grand officers are now some of them officers of particular Lodges; but are not thereby deprived of their priviledge in the Grand Lodge to sit and vote there as old Grand officers; only he deputes one of his particular Lodge to act *pro tempore* as the officer of that Lodge at the quarterly communication.

XVIII. If the Deputy be sick or necessarily absent, the Grand Master can chuse any Brother he pleases to act as his Deputy *pro tempore*, 1.

But he that is chosen Deputy at the installment, and also the Grand Wardens, cannot be discharged, unless the cause fairly appear to the Grand Lodge: for the Grand Master if he is uneasie, may call a Grand Lodge

XVIII. 1. The senior Grand Warden however supplies the Deputy's place; the junior acts as the senior, the oldest former Grand Warden as the junior, Master of a Lodge as mentioned in the 14th old regulation.
2. This was never done in our time.
See new regulation I.

| *Old Regulations.* | *New Regulations.* |

on purpose, to lay the cause before them, for their advice and concurrence. 2

And if the members of the Grand Lodge cannot reconcile the Grand Master with his Deputy or Wardens, they are to allow the Grand Master to discharge his Deputy or wardens, and to chuse another Deputy immediately; and the same Grand Lodge in that case shall forthwith chuse other Grand Wardens; that so harmony and peace peace may be preserved. 3

XIX. And if the Grand Master should abuse his great power, and render himself unworthy of the obedience and subjection of the Lodges, he shall be treated in a way and manner to be agreed upon in a new regulation: because hitherto the antient Fraternity have had no occasion for it.

XX. The Grand Master with his Deputy, Grand Wardens and Secretary, shall at least once go round and visit all the Lodges about town during his Mastership.

3. Should this case ever happen the Grand Master appoints his Deputy, and the Grand Lodge the other Grand officers.

XIX. The Free-Masons firmly hope that there never will be any occasion for such a new regulation.

XX. Or else he shall send his Grand officers to visit the Lodges. This old laudable practice often renders a Deputy necessary: and when he visits them, the senior Grand Warden acts as Deputy, the junior as the senior as above; or if both or any of them be absent, the Deputy or he that presides for him, may appoint whom he pleases in their stead *pro tempore.*

For when both the Grand Masters are absent, the senior

[103]

Old Regulations.

New Regulations.

or junior Grand Warden may preside as Deputy in visiting the Lodges, or in the consitution of a new Lodge; neither of which can be done without, at least, one of the present Grand officers.

XXI. If the Grand Master die during his Mastership, or by sickness or by being beyond sea or any other way should be rendered uncapable of discharging his office, the Deputy or in his absence the senior Grand Warden, or in his absence the junior Grand Warden, or in his absence any three present Masters of Lodges, shall assemble the Grand Lodge immediately; in order to advise together upon that emergency, and to send two of their number to invite the last Grand Master to resume his office, which now of course reverts to him: and if he refuse to act, then the next last, and so backward. But if no former Grand Master be found, the present Deputy shall act as principle till a new Grand Master is chosen: or if there be no Deputy, then the oldest Mason the present Master of a Lodge.

XXI. Upon such a vacancy if no former Grand Master nor former Deputy be found, the present senior Grand Warden fills the Chair, or in his absence the junior till a new Grand Master is chosen: and if no present nor former Grand Warden be found then the oldest Free-Mason who is now the Master of a Lodge.

XXII. The Brethren of all the Lodges in and about the city of *Dublin*, shall meet in some convenient place on every St *John's* day and when business is over, they may repair to their festival

XXII. Or any Brethren around the Globe who are true and faithful, at the place appointed: but none but members of the Grand Lodge are admitted in the doors, during the

Old Regulations.	New Regulations.
dinners as they shall think most convenient; and if St *John's* day at any time shall happen to be on a sunday, then the publick meeting shall be on the day following. The Grand Lodge must meet in some convenient place, on St *John* the Evangelist's day on every year; in order to chuse or recognise a new Grand Master, Deputy, and Grand Wardens. XXIII. If the present Grand Master shall consent to continue for a second year then one of the Grand Lodge Deputed for that purpose shall represent to all the Brethren his worship's good government, &c. and turning to him, shall in the name of the Grand Lodge, humbly request him to do the Fraternity the great honour (if nobly born, if not) the great kindness of continuing to be their Grand Master for the year ensuing: and his worship declaring his consent by a bow or a speech, as he pleases, the said deputed member of the Grand Lodge shall proclaim him aloud. GRAND MASTER OF MASONS! All the members of the Grand Lodge shall salute him in due form; according to the antient and laudable custom of Free Masons. XXIV. The present Grand Master, shall nominate his suc-	time of the election of Grand officers. XXIII. It was agreed that application should be made to the Grand Master by the Deputy, (or such Brother whom the Grand Lodge shall appoint) at least one month before St *John* the Evangelist's day, in order to enquire whether his worship will do the Fraternity the great honour (or kindness) of continuing in his office a second year, or of nominating his successor: and if his worship should at that time happen to be out of town, or the person whom he shall think proper to succeed him; that then the secretary shall write to either concerning the same, a copy of which letter shall be incerted in the transaction book of the Grand Lodge as also the answer received. XXIV. This regulation has always been put in practice in the

[105]

| *Old Regulations.* | *New Regulations.* |

cessor for the year ensuing, who if unanimously approved by the Grand Lodge, and there present, shall be proclaimed saluted, and congratulated the new GRAND MASTER, as above hinted, and immediately installed by the last Grand Master, according to usage.

XXV. But if that nomination is not unanimously approved, the new Grand Master shall be chosen immediately by ballot; every Master and Warden writing his man's name and the last Grand Master writing his man's name too; and the man whose name the last Grand Master shall first take out casually or by chance, shall be

GRAND MASTER OF MASONS

for the year ensuing; and if present, he shall be proclaimed, saluted and congratulated as above hinted, and forthwith installed by the last Grand Master according to usage.

XXVI. The last Grand Master thus continued, or the new Grand Master thus installed, shall next nominate and appoint his Deputy Grand Master either the last or a new one, who shall be also proclaimed, saluted and congratulated in due form.

The new Grand Master shall also nominate his new Grand Wardens; and if unanimously approved by the Grand Lodge, they shall be forthwith pro-

Grand Lodge in *Dublin*.

XXV. There has been no occasion for this old regulation in our time; the Grand Lodge having constantly approved of the Grand Master's choice.

XXVI. A Deputy was always needful when the Grand Master was nobly born: and this old regulation has always been practised in our time.

Old Regulations.	New Regulations.
claimed, saluted, and congratulated in due form.	
But if not they shall be chosen by ballot in the same way as the Grand Master was chosen, and as Wardens of private Lodges are chosen when the members do not approve of their Master's nomination.	
XXVII. But if the Brother whom the present Grand Master shall nominate for his successor or whom the Grand Lodge shall chuse by ballot, as above, is by sickness, or other necessary occasion, absent, he cannot be proclaimed Grand Master; unless the old Grand Master, or some of the Masters and Wardens of Lodges, can vouch upon the honour of a Brother, that the said person, so nominated or chosen, will readily accept the office; in which case the old Grand Master shall act as proxy, and in his name shall receive the usual honours, homage and congratulations.	XXVII. The proxy must be either the last or a former Grand Master; as the Duke of Richmond was for Lord Paisly in *London*, or else a very reputable Brother as Lord Southwell was for the Earl of Strathmore in the same place. But the new Deputy and Grand Wardens are not allowed proxys when appointed.
XXVIII. The Grand Master or Deputy, or some other appointed by him, shall harangue all the Brethren and give them good advice. And lastly after some transactions that cannot be written in any language, the Brethren may stay longer or go away, as they please, when the Lodge is closed in good time.	XXVIII. Other things relating to the charges &c of the Grand Master are best known to the Fraternity.
XXIX. Every annual Grand Lodge has an inherent power	XXIX. The Grand Lodge made the following resolution,

| *Old Regulations.* | *New Regulations.* |

and authority to make new regulations or to alter these for the real benefit of this antient Fraternity, provided always that the old land marks be carefully preserved, and that such new regulations and alterations be proposed and agreed to at the third quarterly communication preceding the annual Grand Lodge; and that they be offered to the perusal of all the Brethren in writing, whose approbation and consent, (or the majority thereof,) is absolutely necessary to make the same binding and obligatory; which must therefore after the new Grand Master is installed be solemnly desired, as it was desired and obtained for these old regulations, by the Grand Lodge, to agreat number of Brethren.

The end of the Old Regulations.

that it is not in the power of any man or body of men to make any innovation in the body of Masonry, without the consent first obtained of the Grand Lodge, and the Grand Lodge when in ample form resolved, that any Grand Lodge duly met has a power to amend or explain any of these printed regulations, while they break not in upon the antient rules of the Fraternity.

ACCORDINGLY

All the alterations or new regulations above written are only for amending or explaining the old regulations for the good of Masonry, without breaking in upon the antient rules of the Fraternity, still preserving the old land marks; and were made at several times as occasion offered, by the Grand Lodge; who have an inherent power of amending what may be thought inconvenient, and ample authority of making new regulations for the good of Masonry; which has not been disputed; for the members of the Grand Lodge are truly the representatives of all the Fraternity, according to old regulation Xth.

The Deputy Grand Master in the Chair proposed the ten following Rules for explaining what concerned the decency of Assemblies and communications, which was agreed to by the Grand Lodges, and are as follows.

XXX. 1. THAT no Brothers be admitted into the Grand Lodge but those that are the known members thereof; that is, The four present and all former Grand officers, the treasurer, and secretary, the Masters and Wardens of all regular Lodges; except a Brother who is a petitioner or witness in some cafe, or one called in by motion.

2. That at the third stroke of the Grand Master's hammer (always to be repeated by the senior Warden) there shall be a general silence; and he who breaks silence without leave from the Chair shall be publickly reprimanded.

3. That under the same penalty every Brother shall take his seat and keep strict silence whenever the Grand Master or Deputy shall think fit to rise from the Chair and call to order.

4. That in the Grand Lodge every member shall keep his seat, and not move about from place to place during the communication; except the Grand Wardens, as having more immediately the care of the Lodge.

5. That according to the order of the Grand Lodge, no Brother is to speak but once to the same affair; unless to explain himself, or when called by the Chair to speak.

6. Every one that speaks shall rise and keep standing, addressing himself to the Chair: nor shall any presume to interrupt him, under the aforesaid penalty; unless the Grand Master, finding his wandering from the point in hand, shall think fit to reduce him to order;

for then the said speaker shall sit down; but after he has been set aright, he may again proceed, if he pleases.

7. If in the Grand Lodge any member is twice called to order, at one assembly, for transgressing these rules, and is guilty of a third offence of the same nature, the Chair shall peremptorily command him to quit the Lodge room for that night.

8. That whoever shall be so rude as to hiss at a Brother, or at what an other says or has said, he shall be solemnly excluded the communication and declared incapable of ever being a member of any Grand Lodge for the future, till another time he publickly owns his fault and his grace be granted.

9. No motion for a new regulation, or for the alteration of an old one shall be made, till it is first handed up in writing to the Chair: and after it has been perused by the Grand Master at least ten minutes, the thing may be moved publickly; and then it shall be audibly read by the secretary; and if he be seconded and thirded, it must be immediately committed to the consideration of the whole assembly, that their sense may be fully heard about it; after which the Grand Master shall put the question pro and con.

10. The opinion or votes of the members are always to be signified by holding up one of his hands; which uplifted the Grand Wardens are to count, unless the numbers of hands be so unequal as to render the counting useless. Nor should any other kind of division be ever admitted among Masons.

The end of the New Regulations.

Some SELECT

SONGS of MASONS.

SONG I.

The FELLOW-CRAFT'S SONG.
By CHARLES DELASAYE, Esq;
To be sung and play'd at the GRAND-FEAST.

I.

HAIL MASONRY! thou *Craft* divine!
   Glory of Earth, from Heav'n reveal'd;
  Which dost with Jewels precious shine,
   From all but *Masons* Eyes conceal'd.

CHORUS.

Thy Praises due who can rehearse
In nervous Prose, or flowing Verse?

II.

As Men from Brutes distinguisht are,
   A *Mason* other Men excels;
For what's in Knowledge choice and rare
   But in his breast securely dwells?

CHORUS.

His silent Breast and faithful Heart
Preserve the Secrets *of the Art.*

III.

From scorching Heat, and piercing Cold;
   From Beasts, whose Roar the Forest rends;
From the Assaults of Warriors bold,
   The *Masons* Art Mankind defends.

CHORUS.

Be to this Art *due Honour paid,*
From which Mankind receives such Aid.

IV.

Ensigns of State, that feed our Pride,
   Distinctions troublesome and vain!
By *Masons* true are laid aside:
   Arts free-born *Sons* such Toys disdain;

CHORUS.

Ennobled by the Name *they bear,*
Distinguisht by the Badge *they wear.*

V.

Sweet Fellowship, from Envy free:
    Friendly Converse of Brotherhood
The *Lodge's* lasting Cement be!
    Which has for Ages firmly stood.

CHORUS.

A Lodge, *thus built, for Ages past*
Has lasted, and will ever last.

VI.

Then in our Songs be Justice done
    To those who have enrich'd the *Art.*
From *Fabal* down to *Burlington,*
    And let each Brother bear a Part.

CHORUS.

Let noble Masons *Healths go round;*
Their Praise in lofty Lodge *resound.*

SONG II.

I.

LET MASONRY be now my Theme,
    Throughout the Globe to spread its Fame,
    And eternize each worthy *Brother's* Name;
Your Praise shall to the Skies resound,
In lasting Happiness abound   (crown'd.
And with sweet Union all your noble Deeds be

CHORUS.

Sing then my Muse to Masons *Glory,*
Your Names are so rever'd in Story,
That all th' admiring World do now adore ye.

II.

Let Harmony Divine inspire
Your Souls with Love and gen'rous Fire,

To copy well wise *Solomon* your Sire;
Knowledge sublime shall fill each Heart
The Rules of *Geometry* t' impart,
Whilst Wisdom, Strength and Beauty crown the
    glorious *Art*.   *Sing, &c.*

III.

Let noble *Allen's* Health go round,
In swelling Cups, all Care be drown'd,
And Hearts united among the *Crafts* be found:
May everlasting Scenes of Joy
His peaceful Hours of Bliss employ,
Which Time's all-conqu'ring Hand, shall ne'er,
    shall ne'er destroy.   *Sing, &c.*

IV.

My *Brethren*, thus all Cares resign,
Your Hearts let glow with Thoughts Divine,
And Veneration show to *Solomon's* Shrine.
Our Annual Tribute thus we'll pay,
That late Posterity shall say,
We've crown'd with Joy this glorious, happy,
    happy Day.   *Sing, &c.*

SONG III.

Tune of, *Near some cool Shade, O let me keep.*

I.

GRANT me kind Heav'n what I request,
    In *Masonry* let me be blest,
    Direct me to that happy Place
Where Friendship smiles in ev'ry Face,
Where Freedom and sweet Innocence
Enlarge the Mind and cheers the Sense.

II.

Where sceptred *Reason* from her Throne
Surveys the *Lodge* and makes us one,

And Harmony's delightful Sway
For ever sheds Ambrosial Day,
Where we blest *Eden's* Pleasures taste,
Whilst balmy Joys are our Repast.

III.

No prying Eye can view us there,
Or Fool or Knave disturb our Cheer.
Our well-form'd Laws set Mankind free
And give Release to Misery.
The Poor, oppress'd with Woe and Grief,
Gain from our bounteous Hands Relief.

IV.

Our Lodge the social Virtues grace,
And Wisdom's Rules we fondly trace,
Whole Nature open to our View
Points out the Paths we should pursue.
Let us subsist in lasting Peace,
And may our Happiness increase.

SONG IV.

I.

ON, on, my dear *Brethren*, pursue the great Lecture,
    And refine on the Rules of old *Architecture*;
High Honour to Masons the *Craft* daily brings,
To these Brothers of Princes, and Fellows of Kings.

II.

We drove the rude *Vandals* and *Goths* off the Stage,
And reviv'd the old Arts of *Augustus'* fam'd Age,
And *Vespasian* destroy'd the vast *Temple* in vain,
Since so many now rise under *George's* blest reign.

III.

Of *Wren* and of *Angelo*, mark the great Names,
Immortal they live as the *Tiber* and *Thames*;

To Heav'n and themselves they such Monuments
    rais'd,
Recorded like *Saints*, and like *Saints* they are prais'd.

IV.

The five noble *Orders* compos'd with such Art,
Shall amaze the fixt Eye, and sink in the Heart;
Proportion's dumb Harmony gracing the whole,
Gives our Work, like the glorious Creation, a Soul.

V.

Then Master and Brethren, preserve your great
    Name;
This *Lodge* so majestick shall purchase you Fame,
Rever'd it shall stand till all Nature expire,
And its Glories ne'er fade till the World is on fire.

VI.

See, see, behold here what rewards all our Toil,
Inspires our Genius, and makes Labour smile;
To our noble *Grand Master* let a Bumper be crown'd,
To all *Masons* a Bumper, so let it go round.

VII.

Again, my lov'd *Brethren*, again let it pass,
Our antient firm Union cements with a Glass,
And all the Contention 'mong *Masons* shall be,
Who better can work, or who better agree.

SONG V.

I.

GUardian *Genius* of our *Art Divine*
    Unto thy faithful Sons appear;
  Cease now o'er Ruins of the *East* to pine,
And smile in blooming Beauties here.

II.

Egypt, *Syria*, and proud *Babylon*
  No more thy blissful Presence claim;

In *Ireland* fix thy ever during Throne,
    Where Myriads do confess thy Name.

III.

The *Sciences* from *Eastern* Regions brought,
    Which after shown in *Greece* and *Rome*,
Are here in several stately *Lodges* taught,
    To which remotest *Brethren* come.

IV.

Behold what strength our rising Domes uprears,
    Till mixing with the azure Skies;
Behold what Beauty through the whole appears,
    So wisely built they must surprise.

V.

Nor are we only to these Arts confin'd,
    For we the Paths of Virtue trace;
By us Man's rugged Nature is refin'd,
    And polish'd into Love and Peace.

SONG VI.

Tune of, *Hark! away, 'tis the merry ton'd Horn*.

I.

SING to the Honour of those
    Who Baseness and Error oppose;
    Who from Sages and Magi of old
Have got *Secrets* which none can unfold,
   Whilst thro' Life's swift Career
   With Mirth and good Cheer
      We're Revelling
      And Levelling
   The Monarch, till he
Says our Joys far transcend
What on Thrones do attend,
And thinks it a Glory like us to be free,

II.

The wisest of Kings pav'd the way,
And its Precepts we keep to this Day;
The most glorious of Temples gave Name
To *Free-Masons*, who still keep their Fame,
   Tho' no Prince did arise
   So great and so wife,
     Yet in falling
       Yet in falling
       Our Calling
   Sill bore high Applause.
And tho' Darkness o'er-run
   The Face of the Sun,
We Diamond-like blaz'd to illumine the Cause.

SONG VII.

Tune of, *Young* Damon *once the hapy Swtin*.

I.

A *Mason's* Daughter fair and young,
   The Pride of all the Virgin Throng,
   Thus to her Lover said;
Tho' *Damon* I your Flame approve,
Your Actions praise, your Person Love,
   Yet still I'll live a Maid.

II.

None shall untye my Virgin Zone,
But one to whom the *Secret's* known
   Of fam'd *Free-Masonry*:
In which the Great and Good combine
To raise, with generous Design,
   Man to Felicity.

III.

The *Lodge* excludes the Fop and Fool,
The plodding Knave and party Tool
   That Liberty would fell:

The Noble, Faithful, and the Brave
No Golden Charms can e'er deceive
  In Slavery to dwell.

IV.

This said, he bow'd, and went away,
Apply'd, was made without Delay,
  Reurn'd to her again.
The Fair One granted his Request,
Connubial Joys their Days have blest;
  And may they e'er remain,

SONG VIII.

SOME Folks have with curious Impertinence (strove
From the *Free-Masons* Bosom their Secrets to move
I'll tell why in vain their Endeavours must prove.
  Which no Body can deny.

II.

Of that happy Secret when we are possest,
Our Tongues can't explain what is lodg'd in our breast:
For the Blessing's so great it can e'er be express'd.
  Which no Body, &c.

III.

By Friendship's strict Tyes we Brothers are join'd,
With Mirth in each Heart, and Content in each Mind;
And this is a difficult Secret to find.
  Which no Body, &c.

IV.

Truth, Charity, Justice, our Principles are,
What one doth possess, the other may share;
All these in the World are Secrets most rare.
  Which no Body, &c.

V.

But you who wou'd fain our grand Secret expose,
One thing best conceal'd, to the World you disclose,
Much Folly in blaming what none of you knows.
Which no Body, &c.

VI.

While then we are met, the World's Wonder and
And all now enjoy what pleases each most, (Boast,
I'll give you the best and most glorious Toast.
Which no Body, &c.

VII.

Her's a Health to the *Generous*, *Brave* and the *Good*,
To all those who think, and who do as they shou'd:
In all this the *Free-Masons* Health's understood.
Which no Body, &c.

A List of the regular Lodges in the City of Dublin, together with the Names of the respective Masters and Wardens, their times and places of meeting.

No. 1. Is at this time vacant.

2. At the Green Posts in Meath-Street every other Monday, Samuel Gilbert Master, Matthew Downs and Jos. Collins Wardens.

3. Lebeck's-head in Dame-Street every other Wednesday.

4. At the Black Lion Draper's Court every other Wednesday. Henry Crostwaight Master, Alexander Richards and William Shaw Wardens.

5. At the Bull's head New-Row on the Poddle every other Monday, William Ray Master, John Downs and Archibold McMullen Wardens.

6. At Mr. Bray's in Ash-Street over against Engine-Alley, Jeremiah Bubb Master, Benjamin Smith and John Bray Wardens.

7. At the White Lion, George's-Lane every other Thursday, Alexander Eakins Master, Peter Butterton and Charles Nappier Wardens.

8. At the Plume of Feathers in Castle-Street.

10. At the Golden Anchor Sycamore-Alley every other Monday, James Delap Master, John Kelly and John Ledgerwood Wardens.

54. At Mr. Russell Church's Street every other Monday, John Foster Master, John Keering and Wiliam Richy Wardens.

86. In Barrack-Street Jos. Coles Master, William Bresington and Thomas Jones Wardens.

97. At the White-Hart Crane-Lane every other Friday, Thomas Hayford Master, Thomas Shepherd and Richard Allen Wardens.

100. At the Black-Lion Park-Street every other Monday, Jos. Cock Master, John Siddon and Edward Stammers Wardens.

105. At the Cock in Warburgh-Street every other Friday, Osborn Barker Master, John Duncan and Robert Finlay Wardens.

133. At Mr. Reading's in Smith-field every other Thursday, Samuel White Master, Allan Reading and John Nicholls Wardens.

137. At Mr. Bray's Swan-Alley every other Tuesday, Edward Dillon Master, John McCaroll and Richard Byrke Wardens.

141. At the Struggler in Cook-Street every other Monday Mr. Patrick Weldon Master, Thomas Millwood and Patrick Caufield Wardens.

F I N I S.

This Plate is Humbly Dedicated to the Right Hon.ble Henry Barnwal Lord Visr Kingsland Grand Master of ye Most Ancient & Right Worshipfull Fraternity of Free and Accepted Masons

A Pocket Companion FOR FREE-MASONS.

CONTAINING

I. The *History* of *Masonry*.
II. The *Charges* of a *Free-Mason*, &c.
III. General Regulations for the Use of the LODGES in and about the City of *Dublin*.
IV. The Manner of constituting a *New Lodge*, according to the antient Usage of *Masons*.
V. A *Short Charge* to be given to a new admitted *Brother*.
VI. A Collection of the Songs of *Masons*, both Old and New.
VII. *Prologues* and *Epilogues*, spoken at the *Theatres* in *Dublin* and *London* for the Entertainment of FREE-MASONS.
VIII. A List of the warranted *Lodges* in *Ireland*, *Great-Britain*, *France*, *Spain*, *Germany*, *East* and *West Indies*, &c.

Approved of, and Recommended by the Grand-Lodge.

Deus nobis Sol & Scutum.

DUBLIN:

Printed by E. RIDER, and sold at the *Printing-Office* in *George's-Lane*; T. JONES in *Clarendon-street*; and J. PENNEL at the *Hercules* in *St. Patrick-street*. M.DCC.XXXV.

TO THE
BRETHREN and FELLOWS
OF THE
Most Antient and Right Worshipful
SOCIETY
OF
FREE and ACCEPTED
MASONS

Worshipful Brethren,

THE great Increase of our *Society* of late, gives us a very pleasing Prospect of having even in our own Days the

Arts

DEDICATION.

Arts of the fam'd *Augustan Age* revive amongst us, and shine in as great Splendour as they did then. What great Things now will not the World expect from us, when they see the Noble, the Learned, and the Wise coming from all Quarters to be received by us, and that we still keep true to our *Grand Principles.* Which that we may always do, is the sincere Wish of

Your loving BROTHER,

And most obedient Servant,

W. S.

THE
PREFACE

AT the Desire of a great many of the Brethren *I have compriz'd the* History, Charges, Regulations, Songs, Account of Lodges, *and several other Articles in* Masonry, *for the most Part extracted from our excellent* Constitution Book, *and not to be found in any one of our Books yet published, in a small Volume easily portable, which will render what was before difficult to come at, and troublesome to carry about, of more extensive Use. For it has been often remark'd that great Numbers, especially of the younger* Masons, *(who have been desirous of knowing every thing relating to the* Craft*) have been a long time frustrated in their Pursuits for want of something of this Kind, which they might have recourse to at any time. I need not say more in relation to the Book itself, but must here beg leave to exhort the* Brotherhood, *that avoiding all Innovations they adhere strictly to the antient Practices of the* Order *when all the social Virtues shone conspicuously amongst us, and the World admired us rather for our Veracity, Brotherly Love, and Relief of one another, than for those invaluable Secrets which we have ever kept, or those Fabricks which we have erected for the Convenience of Mankind and Ornament of the World.*

The PREFACE

Let it never be said, that as our Numbers increase the Sciences decrease, but let our Knowledge shine as formerly for our own Honour and the Edification of others. No Man ought to attain to any Dignity in Masonry, *who has not, as least, a competent Knowledge in* Geometry and Architecture; *and if the Sciences were more follow'd in the* Lodges, *what is unhappily substituted in their Places would not prevail as it does. Then let us all go Hand in Hand in promoting the great and laudable Ends of our Institution, and we cannot fail of gaining the Approbation of the whole World as well as of one another.*

A POCKET COMPANION FOR FREE-MASONS.

The History of MASONRY.

BY *Geometry*, which is the Basis of MASONRY as well as of all other Sciences, we trace out the Wisdom, Strength and Beauty display'd in all the wondrous Works of the great Author of Nature, and thence with adoration reflect them to their all-wise, all-potent and most amiable Origin. From this Contemplation of the divine Perfection, we are naturally led to be Imitators thereof, and whoever comes nighest to this glorious Pattern is undoubtedly the most excellent in the Train of human Agency. Our first Father *Adam* was left without excuse, when he transgress'd the Divine Command, as having this unerring Rule to direct him, without any Seeds of Corruption in his Body of jarring Principles in his Mind; but after his Default the Passions usurp'd the Throne of Reason, lately their Master, and thro' his unhappy Race have but too much born the sway. New Appetites arose, and several things became necessary for him which were not so before. Hence that Time and Science which should have been applied to the Contemplation of the Works of God and the pursuit of his own Perfection, was almost entirely taken up in the invention and making of what might defend him from the Inclemencies of the Weather, and Dangers of the brutal World, now at war with him. Happy still in this, that God had not withdrawn from him his knowledge in *Geometry*, by which he and his immediate Descendants invented several curious Arts, which have not been lost to this Day, but have all along been the Glory of Mankind, and an Ornament to the World.

We may be very well assured, that *Adam* instructed his Descendants in *Geometry* and the application of it, to whatever Crafts were convenient for those early Times. For *Cain* built a City, which he called after the Name of his eldest Son *Enoch*; and his Posterity following his example, improved not only in *Geometry* and MASONRY, but made Discoveries of several other curious Arts, as the way of working in Mettal by *Tubal Cain*, Musick by *Jubal*, Pastorage, Tent-making and building in Stone and Timber by *Jabal*.

Nor is it to be suppos'd that the Descendants of *Seth*, who first taught Astronomy, came any thing behind those of *Cain* in the cultivation of *Geometry* and MASONRY. For *Enoch* the fifth from *Seth* (who prophecy'd of the Deluge and final Conflagration) erected two Piliars, the one of Stone and the other of Brick, whereon he engraved the liberal Sciences, &c. And the Stone Pillar remained in *Syria* until the Days of the Emperor *Vespasian*.

The first Piece of MASONRY that we know of, under Divine Direction, was that of *Noah's* Ark, wherein *Noah* and his three Sons *Japhet*, *Shem* and *Ham*, all *Masons* true, were preserv'd from Destruction, and afterwards communicated to their Children, *Geometry*, and the Art of Building; for we find that about 110 Years after the Flood, great numbers of them assembled in the Plains of *Shinar* to build a City and a large Tower, in order to make themselves a Name, and prevent their Dispersion; but God, for their Vanity by confounding their Speech, occasion'd that which they endeavour'd to avoid. Yet they still carried with them the knowledge of MASONRY; for *Nimrod*, the Founder of the *Assyrian* Monarchy, after the general Dispersion, built the Cities of *Nineveh*, *Rehoboth*, and many others. And the learned Mathematicians in those Parts, who were called Magi, cultivated both *Geometry* and

MASONRY, under the Patronage of the Kings and great Men of the *East*.

The Confusion of Tongues hindred not the Improvement of MASONRY in their several Colonies; for the Descendants of *Shem* in *Asia*, of *Ham* in *Africa*, and of *Japhet* in *Europe*, left behind them sufficient Vestiges to demonstrate their great Skill in MASONRY. But of these, the *Assyrians* and *Egyptians* seem'd to have made the greatest Progress in the Royal Art, as the Walls of *Babylon* and the Pyramids of *Egypt* evidently shew, which were two of the Seven Wonders of the World.

Here we must not forget the glorious Temple of *Diana* at *Ephesus*, one of the Wonders, which was finish'd under the Direction of the Master Masons *Dresiphon* and *Archiphron*; nor the Tomb of *Mausolus*, King of *Caria*, another of the Wonders, which was built with great magnificence, by order of his sorrowful Widow *Artemisia*, and performed by the four great Master Masons of that Age, viz. *Leochares*, *Briax*, *Scopas*, and *Timotheus*.

The Descendants of the great *Abraham*, who taught the *Egyptians* the Learning of the *Assyrians*, being only Sojourners and Shepherds in *Egypt*, practised very little of the Architecture, except the building of Tents, till about 86 Years before their *Exodus*, when by the over-ruling Hand of Providence they were trained up to building in Stone and Brick, in order to make them good *Masons* before they possessed the promised Land, then famous for good *Masonry*.

And during this Peregrination in the Wilderness of *Arabia*, the inspired *Bezaleel* and *Aholiab* erected the most glorious Tabernacle, which proved afterwards the Model of *Solomon's* Temple, according to the Pattern which God gave *Moses* in the Mount, who then became the *Grand Master Mason* of the Lodge of *Israel*, to which he gave wise *Charges* and *Orders*, &c.

The *Israelites* continued to improve in *Geometry*, and even to exceed the *Canaanites*; for the magnificent Temple of *Dagon*, destroy'd by *Sampson*, and the other most noted Structures of the Earth, came infinitely short of the glorious Temple of G O D at *Jerusalem*, which was built by the most wise and magnificent King *Solomon* the Son of *David*, without the noise of Workmen's Tools. In this stupendous Work were employ'd 3600 Princes or *Master*

Masons to conduct the Work, with 80,000 Hewers of Stone in the Mountain, and 70,000 Labourers, which with the Levy of 30,000 under *Adoniram* to work by turns with the *Sidonians* in the Mountains of *Lebanon*, makes the whole number to amount to 183,600.

This most splendid Temple, to the amazement of the World, was begun and finish'd at an almost uncredible Expence, in the short Space of seven Years and six Months. The Wall that surrounded it was 7700 Feet in compass, and its Courts and Apartments were capable of receiving 300,000 People. It had 1453 Columns, and 2906 Pillasters of Parian Marble, with glorious Capitals, and about 2246 Windows. These, with the most gorgeous and costly Decorations within, together with the convenient and lovely Apartments for the Kings, the Princes and Priests, &c. make us justly esteem it, by far the finest Piece of MASONRY upon Earth, and the chief Wonder of the World.

This glorious Edifice thus built under the Care and Direction of Heaven (King *Solomon* being Grand Master of the Lodge at *Jerusalem* and the inspired *Hiram Abif*, Master of the Work) became the Wonder of all Travellers; by which, as by the most perfect Pattern, they corrected the Architecture of their own Countries upon their return, and improved MASONRY in all the neighbouring Nations. The Kings, Princes and Potentates becoming Grand Masters each in his own Territory, many glorious Fabricks were erected, of which, some Vestiges still remaining, declare their magnificence. But neither the stupendous Walls, Temples and Palaces erected by *Nebuchadnezzar* at *Babylon*, the Temple of *Diana* at *Ephesus*, nor all the most famous Edifices in *Asia*, *Egypt*, *Greece*, or *Rome*, in the Perfection of MASONRY, could ever compare with the holy, charming Temple of GOD at *Jerusalem*.

In 416 Years after the finishing of this Temple, it was destroyed by *Nebuchadnezzar*, King of *Assyria*, and the remainder of the *Jews* carried Captive to *Babylon*; but upon their return, under the Reign of the great *Cyrus*, they built another Temple, commonly called the Temple of *Zorobbabel*, which tho' a stupendous Fabrick, came infinitely short of the first. Many Ages after which, *Herod* built a third Temple, which was erected and finished in 43 Years with very great Magnificence, which Temple was afterwards burnt by the factious *Jews*, upon the taking of the Temple by *Titus Vespasian*.

After the erecting of the Temple of *Solomon*, but more especially after that of *Zorobbabel*, the *Grecians* brought the *Royal Art* into their Country, and erected several noble Structures, as the Cittadel of *Athens*, the Temples of *Minerva*, *Theseus* and *Jupiter Olympius*, their Halls, Portico's, Forums, Gymnasiums, and stately Palaces, some Vestiges of which remain to this Day. But the *Grecians* were never remarkable for any great Skill in *Geometry* till the time of *Thales Milesius* and his Scholar *Pythagoras*, who was the Author of the 47th Proposition of the first Book of *Euclid*, which if rightly understood, is the Foundation of all MASONRY.

The admirable *Euclid* of *Tyre*, who flourished at *Alexandria* under the Patronage of *Ptolomeus*, the Sons of *Lagus*, King of *Egypt*, gathered the scatter'd Elements of *Geometry*, and digested them into a Method never yet mended.

The next King of *Egypt*, *Ptolomeus Philadelphus*, that great improver of all useful Knowledge, (who gathered the greatest Library upon Earth) erected among other great Buildings, the famous Lighthouse or Tower of *Pharos*, one of the Seven Wonders of the World.

The *Romans* from *Sicily* (where the great Geometrician *Archimedes* flourished) as well as from *Asia*, *Egypt* and *Greece*, received the liberal Sciences. And in the Reign of *Augustus Caesar* (when the Glory of the *Roman* Empire was advanced to its Zenith) was *CHRIST* the great Architect of the Church born, who proclaiming universal Peace, gave opportunity to the famous Architects of that time, of making many Improvements in the noble Arts, and erecting several stately Edifices, the remains of which are the Pattern and Standard of true *Masonry* at this very Day, as the great *Vitruvius* who then flourished, is esteemed the Father of all our modern Architects, who are but endeavouring as yet to imitate the *Augustan Stile* in their Performances.

Masonry continued to flourish till about the fifth Century, when a Deluge of *Goths* and *Vandals* overrun the Empire; who destroying most of the antient *Roman* Buildings introduced their own confus'd Architecture, which with very little knowledge in *Geometry*, prevailed in the World till the fifteenth and sixteenth Centuries, when the *Augustan Stile* began to revive in *Italy* by the Endeavours of *Bramante, Brabaro, Michael Angelo, Raphael Urbin, Scamozzi, Vignola,* and other Architects, more especially the great *Palladio,* who has been justly rival'd in *England,* by our famous Master Mason *Inigo Jones.*

The *Gothic* Architecture was much encouraged in *England,* even in the time of the *Heptarchy;* at which time *Charles Martel,* King of *France,* sent over several expert Architects and Craftsmen at the Request of the *Saxon* Kings. But for the farther Instruction of new admitted Brethren, a certain Record of FREE MASONS, written in the Reign of King *Edward* IV, gives the following Account, *viz.*:

> "That tho' the antient Records of the Brotherhood in *England,* were many of them destroy'd or lost in the Wars of the *Saxons* and *Danes,* yet *King Athelstan,* (the Grandson of King *Alfred the Great* a mighty Architect) the first anointed King of *England,* and who translated the Holy Bible into the *Saxon* Tongue; when he had brought the Land into Rest and Peace, built many great Works, and encouraged many *Masons* from *France,* who were appointed Overseers thereof, and brought with them the Charges and Regulations of the Lodges preserved since the *Roman* Times, who also prevailed with the King to improve the Constitution of the *English* Lodges according to the foreign Model, and to increase the Wages of working *Masons.*
>
> "That the said King's youngest Son, Prince *Edwin,* being taught *Masonry,* and taking upon him the Charges of a Master Mason, for the love he had to the said *Craft,* and the honourable Principles whereon it is grounded, purchased a free Charter of King *Athelstan* his Father; for the *Masons* having a Correction amongst themselves, (as it was antiently express'd) or a Freedom and Power to regulate themselves, to amend what might happen amiss, and to hold a yearly Communication and general Assembly.
>
> "That accordingly Prince *Edwin* summoned all the *Masons* in the Realm to meet him in a Congregation at *York,* who came and composed a general Lodge, of which he was Grand Master; and having brought with them all the Writings and Records extant, some in *Greek,* some in *Latin,* some in *French,* and other Languages, from the Contents thereof that Assembly did frame the Constitution and Charges of an *English* Lodge, made a Law to preserve and observe the fame in all time coming, and ordained good Pay for the working *Masons,* &c.
>
> "That in process of time, when the Lodges were more frequent, the

Right Worshipful the Master and Fellows, with the consent of the Lords of the Realm (for most great Men were then *Masons*) ordained, That for the future, at the Making or Admission of a Brother, the Constitution should be read, and the Charges hereunto annexed, by the Master or Warden; and that such as were to be admitted Master Masons, or Masters of Work, should be examined whether they be able of Cunning to serve their respective Lords, as well the lowest as the highest, to the Honour and Worship of the aforesaid Act, and to the Profit of their Lords; for they be their Lords that employ and pay them for their Service and Travel."

And besides many other Things, the said Record adds:

"That those Charges and Laws of FREE MASONS have been seen and perused by our late Sovereign King *Henry* VI, and by the Lords of his Honourable Council, who have allowed them, and said that they be right good and reasonable to be holden, as they have been drawn out and collected from the Records of antient Times."

The *Augustan Stile* was revived in *England* by King *James* the First, who employed the great *Inigo Jones* in building him a Palace at *Whitehall*, which if it had been finished, would, in every Perfection of *Masonry*, have exceeded all the Palaces of the known Earth. This was afterwards carried on by King *Charles* the First, another Mason King; but the unhappy *Civil Wars* caused this glorious Design to drop; yet the stately Banquetting House, now a Chapel, remains a Monument of its design'd Grandeur.

In the Reign of the next Mason King, *Charles* the Second, several noble Fabricks in the antient *Roman* Taste began to appear. This King founded and finished his Royal Palace of *Holy-Rood-House* which has been esteemed the finest House belonging to the Crown. He founded the Royal Hospital at *Chelsea*, a Palace at *Greenwich*, as also St. *Paul's* Church, after the Stile of St. *Peter's* at *Rome*, conducted by that excellent Architect, Sir *Christopher Wren*.

In the Reign of King *William*, who is with good reason believed to have been a *Free Mason*, the Hospitals of *Greenwich* and *Chelsea* were carried on; the fine Buildings at *Hampton-Court* erected; the beautiful Palace of *Loo* in *Holland* built; and in fine, this Prince by his example gave such a turn of Taste to the *English* Nation, that ever since his time the Nobility and Gentry of *England* join, as it were, hand in hand, with generous Ambition, in pursuit of the Beauty and Elegance of the antient Architecture.

His immediate Successor, the glorious Queen *Ann*, proved a great Encourager of the *Royal Art*; in the Ninth Year of whose Reign there was an Act of Parliament passed for the Building of 50 new Churches in *London* and *Westminster*, all in the *Augustan Stile*.

These were carried on by King *George* the First, who by Proxy laid the first Stone of the Church of *St. Martin's in the Fields*, a fair and strong Building, conducted by Mr. *Gibbs*, a noted Architect.

In the Reign of his present Majesty *Masonry* flourishes very much, and several fine Buildings have been finished, and others now carrying on. And, indeed, it may be said to the Glory of the *English* Masons, that there are but few Nations in the World than can equal *England* in the Number of fine Edifices, and it continues still to increase in them; that great Architect, the Earl of *Burlington*, Mr. *Kent*, the ingenious Mr. *Flitcroft* who conducted the Building of the new Church of *St. Giles's in the Fields* (an elegant Structure) with many other excellent Architects now living, using their unwearied Endeavours for the Improvement of *Masonry* and Ornament of the Kingdom.

The Number of *Lodges* has prodigeously encreased within these few Years in *Great Britain* and *Ireland*; and it is to be hoped, that *Geometry* and the *Royal Art* will be inculcated in every one of them.

In *IRELAND*, a Country once the most famous of any for Learning*, there are several stately Remains of the antient Grandeur of the *Irish*, shewn in the Ruins of several magnificently extructed Churches, Monasteries, Castles, and other Buildings; and at this Day, notwithstanding all the Disadvantages under which that Kingdom labours, Learning and Arts hold up their Heads, and several noble Churches, Hospitals, and other Edifices bespeak the publick Spirit of the *Irish*.

In *Dublin* is a noble Palace, where the Lord-Lieutenant keeps

---

* *Cambden* observes, that the *Saxons* formerly flock'd to *Ireland*, as to the great Mart of Learning; and *Bede* and other *English* Authors frequently take notice of the *Saxons* sending their Sons thither, for Education. We likewise find, in the Life of St. *Senan*, that he being in his Island of *Cathay*, "a Ship arrived there bringing some Monks, for there were expected 50 Monks, *Romans* by Birth, who were drawn into *Ireland* by the Desire of a stricter Life, or Skilfulness in the Scriptures, which then much flourish'd there."

his Court; a stately Tholsel; a magnificent Hospital for old or decrepid Soldiers; a Work-house not inferior to any of those in *Holland*; a fine new Building, call'd Dr. *Steven's* Hospital; a Custom-house admired by all that see it; a Barracks for Horse and Foot, the most magnificent, largest and most comodious of the kind in *Europe*; and a College, which to the immortal Honour of *Ireland*, has given Education to some of the greatest Genius's that have shined in the World of Letters, the Building of which is so large and beautiful withal, that scarce any thing of the kind can come up to it, and its Library for length and stateliness surpassing all others.

The Parliament House where the great Senate of the Realm assembles, is built in the true *Italian* Taste, and is not only one of the chief Ornaments of the Kingdom, but, perhaps, the stateliest of the kind upon Earth. This noble Building was conducted by the ingenuous Captain *Pierce*, Successor to the famous Architect, *Bourk*, under whole direction most of the fine Buildings about *Dublin* were erected.

I might here enumerate several other fine Edifices which adorn this City and Kingdom as the Churches, Houses of the Nobility, publick Schools; Bridges, &c. but that I should then exceed my designed Brevity. May the whole *Brotherhood*, wheresoever dispersed, continue thus to adorn the World; may Learning and Arts flourish, and Brotherly Love subsist amongst them, till Time shall be no more.

The CHARGES *of a* FREE-MASON, *to be read at the making of new* Brethren, *or when the* Master *Shall order it.*

The General Heads, viz.

I. Of *God* and *Religion*.
II. Of the *Civil Magistrate* supreme and subordinate.

III. Of *Lodges*.
IV. Of *Masters, Wardens, Fellows,* and *Apprentices.*
V. Of the Management of the *Craft* in Working.
VI. Of *Behaviour*, viz.

1. In the *Lodge* while *constituted.*
2. After the *Lodge* is over and the *Brethren* not gone.
3. When Brethren meet without *Strangers*, but not in a *Lodge.*
4. In Presence of *Strangers not Masons.*
5. At *Home*, and in the *Neighbourhood.*
6. Towards a *strange Brother.*

I. *Concerning* God *and* Religion

A *Mason* is obliged, by his Tenure, to obey the Moral Law; and if he rightly understands the Art, he will never be a stupid *Atheist*, nor an irreligious *Libertine*. But tho' in antient Times *Masons* were charged in every Country to be of the Religion of that Country or Nation, whatever it was, yet it is now thought more expedient only to oblige them to that Religion in which all Men agree, leaving their particular opinions to themselves; that is, to be *good Men and true*, or Men of Honour and Honesty, by whatever Denominations or Persuasions they may be distinguish'd; whereby *Masonry* become the Centre of Union, and the means of conciliating true Friendship among Persons that must have remain'd at a perpetual Distance.

II. *Of the* Civil Magistrate *Supreme and Subordinate.*

A *Mason* is a peaceable Subject to the Civil Powers, wherever he resides or works, and is never to be concerned in Plots and Conspiracies against the Peace and Welfare of the Nation, nor to behave himself undutifully to inferior Magistrates; for as *Masonry* hath been always injured by War, Bloodshed, and Confusion, so antient Kings and Princes have been much disposed to encourage the *Craftsmen*, because of their *Peaceableness* and *Loyalty*, whereby they practically answer'd the Cavils of their Adversaries, and promoted the Honour of the Fraternity, who ever flourish'd in Times of Peace. So that if a Brother should be a Rebel against the State, he is not to be countenanced in his Rebellion, however he may be pitied as an unhappy Man; and, if convicted of no other Crime, tho' the loyal Brotherhood must and ought to disown his Rebellion, and give no Umbrage or Ground of political Jealousy to the Government for the time being; they cannot expel him from the *Lodge* and his Relation to it remains indefeasible.

III. *Of* Lodges.

A *Lodge* is a Place where *Masons* assemble and work: Hence that Assembly, or duly organiz'd Society of *Masons*, is call'd a *Lodge*, and every Brother ought to belong to one, and to be subject to its *By-Laws* and the *General Regulations*. It is either particular or general, and will be best understood by attending it, and by the Regulations of the *General* or *Grand Lodge* hereunto annexed. In antient Times, no Master or Fellow could be absent from it, especially when warn'd to appear at it, without incurring a severe Censure, until it appeared to the Master and Wardens, that pure Necessity hinder'd him.

The Persons admitted Members of a *Lodge* must be good and true Men, free-born, of mature and discreet Age, no Bondmen, no Women, no immoral or scandalous Men, but of good Report.

IV. *Of* Masters, Wardens, Fellows, *and* Apprentices.

All Preferment among *Masons* is grounded upon real Worth and personal Merit only; that so the the *Lords* may be well served, the Brethren not put to Shame, nor the *Royal Craft* despited: Therefore no Master or Warden is chosen by Seniority, but for his Merit. It is impossible to describe these things in Writing, and every Brother must attend in his Place, and learn them in a way peculiar to *this Fraternity*: Only Candidates may know, that no Master should take an Apprentice, unless he has sufficient Employment, for him, and unless he be a perfect Youth, having no Maim or Defect in his Body, that might render him uncapable of learning the *Art*, of serving his Master's Lord, and of being made a Brother, and then a Fellow-Craft in due time, even after he has served such a Term of Years as the Custom of the Country directs; and that he should be descended of honest Parents; that so, when otherwise qualified, he may arrive to the Honour of being the Warden, and then Master of the *Lodge*, the Grand Warden, and, at length the Grand Master of all the *Lodges*, according to his Merit.

No Brother can be a Warden until he has pass'd the Part of Fellow-Craft; nor a Master until he has acted as a Warden, nor Grand-Warden until he has been Master of a *Lodge*, nor Grand-Master unless he has been a Fellow-Craft before his Election, who is also to be nobly born, or a Gentleman of the best fashion, or some eminent Scholar, or some curious Architect, or other Artist, descended of honest Parents, and who is of singular great Merit in the Opinion of the *Lodges*. And for the better, and easier, and more honourable Discharge of his Office, the Grand-Master has a Power to chuse his own Deputy Grand-Master, who must be then, or must have been formerly, the Master of a particular *Lodge*, and has the privilege of acting whatever the Grand-Master, his Principal, should act, unless the said Principal be present, or interpose his Authority by a Letter.

These Rulers and Governors, supreme and subordinate, of the antient *Lodge*, are to be obeyed in their respective Stations by all the Brethren, according to the *old Charges and Regulations*, with all Humility, Reverence, Love, and Alacrity.

V. *Of the Management of the* Craft *in working.*

All *Masons* shall work honestly on working Days that they may live creditably on *Holy Days*; and the time appointed by the Law of the Land, or confirm'd by Custom, shall be observed.

The most expert of the Fellow-Craftsmen shall be chosen or appointed the Master, or Overseer of the Lord's Work; who is to be call'd Master by those that work under him. The Craftsmen are to avoid all ill Language, and to call each other by no disobliging Name, but Brother or Fellow; and to behave themselves courteously within and without the *Lodge*.

The Master, knowing himself to be able of Cunning, shall undertake the Lord's Work as reasonably as possible, and truly dispend his Goods as if they were his own; nor to give more Wages to any Brother or Apprentice than he really may deserve.

Both the Master and the Masons receiving their Wages justly, shall be faithful to the Lord, and honestly finish their Work, whether Task or Journey; nor put the Work to Task that hath been accustomed to Journey.

None shall discover Envy at the Prosperity of a Brother, nor supplant him, or put him out of his Work, if he be capable to finish the same; for no Man can finish another's Work so much to the Lord's Profit, unless he be thoroughly acquainted with the Designs and Draughts of him that began it.

When a Fellow-Craftsman is chosen Warden of the Work under the Master, he shall be true both to Master and Fellows, shall carefully oversee the Work in the Master's Absence to the Lord's Profit; and his Brethren shall obey him.

All Masons employ'd shall meekly receive their Wages without Murmuring or Mutiny, and not desert the Master till the Work is finish'd.

A younger Brother shall be instructed in working, to prevent spoiling the Materials for want of Judgment, and for encreasing and continuing of Brotherly Love.

All the Tools used in working shall be approved by the Grand Lodge.

No Labourer shall be employed in the proper Work of *Masonry*, nor shall *Free-Masons* work with those that are *not free*, without an urgent Necessity; nor shall they teach Labourers and unaccepted Masons, as they should teach a Brother or Fellow.

VI. *Of* Behaviour, *viz.*

1. *In the* Lodge *while constituted.*

You are not to hold private Committees, or separate Conversation, without Leave from the Master, nor to talk of any Thing impertinent or unseemly, nor interrupt the Master or Wardens, or any Brother speaking to the Master: Nor behave yourself ludicrously or jestingly while the *Lodge* is engaged in what is serious and solemn; nor use any unbecoming Language upon any Pretence whatsoever; but to pay due Reverence to your Master, Wardens, and Fellows, and put them to worship.

If any Complaint be brought, the Brother found guilty shall stand to the Award and Determination of the *Lodge*, who are the proper and competent Judges of all such Controversies, (unless you carry it by *Appeal* to the *Grand Lodge*) and to whom they ought to be referr'd, unless a Lord's Work be hinder'd the mean while, in which Case a particular Reference may be made; but you must never go to Law about what concerneth *Masonry*, without an absolute Necessity apparent to the *Lodge*.

2. Behaviour *after the* Lodge *is over and the* Brethren *not gone.*

You may enjoy yourselves with innocent Mirth, treating one another according to Ability, but avoiding all Excess or forcing any Brother to eat or drink beyond his Inclination, or hindering him from going when his Occasions call him, or doing or saying any thing offensive, or that may forbid an easy and free Conversation; for that would blast our Harmony, and defeat our laudable Purposes. Therefore no private Picques or Quarrels must be brought within the Door of the *Lodge*, far less any Quarrels about *Religion*, or *Nations*, or *State Policy*, we being only, as *Masons*, of the *Catholick Religion* above-mention'd; we are also of all *Nations, Tongues, Kindreds*, and *Languages*, and are resolv'd against all *Politicks*, as what never yet conduced to the Welfare of the *Lodge*, nor ever will. This *Charge* has been always strictly enjoined and observed; but especially ever since the *Reformation* in *Britain*, or the Dissent and Secession of these Nations from the Communion of *Rome*.

3. Behaviour *when* Brethren *meet without* Strangers, *but not in a* Lodge *form'd.*

You are to salute one another in a courteous manner, as you will be instructed, calling each other *Brother*, freely giving mutual Instructions as shall be thought expedient, without being overseen or overheard, and without encroaching upon each other, or derogating from that Respect which is due to any Brother, were he not a Mason; for tho' all *Masons* are as Brethren upon the same *Level*, yet *Masonry* takes no Honour from a Man that he had before; nay rather it adds to his Honour, especially if he has deserved well of the Brotherhood, who must give Honour to whom it is due, and avoid ill Manners.

4. Behavior *in Presence of Strangers not* Masons.

You shall be cautious in your Words and Carriage, that the most penetrating Stranger shall not be able to discover or find out what is not proper to be intimated; and sometimes you shall divert a Discourse, and manage it prudently for the Honour of the *Worshipful Fraternity*.

5. Behaviour *at Home and in your Neighbourhood*.

You are to act as becomes a moral and wise Man; particularly, not to let your Family, Friends, and Neighbours know the *Concerns* of the *Lodge, &c.* but wisely to consult your own Honour, and that of the *antient Brotherhood*, for Reasons not to be mentioned here. You must also consult your Health, by not continuing together too late, or too long from home, after Lodge Hours are past; and by avoiding of Gluttony or Drunkenness, that your Families be not neglected or injured, nor you disabled from working.

6. Behaviour *towards a Strange* Brother.

You are cautiously to examin him, in such a Method as Prudence shall direct you, that you may not be impos'd upon by an ignorant false *Pretender*, whom you are to reject with Contempt and Derision, and beware of giving him any Hints of Knowledge.

But if you discover him to be a true and genuine *Brother*, you are to respect him accordingly; and if he is in want, you must relieve him if you can, or else direct him how he may be relieved: You must employ him some Days, or else recommend him to be employed. But you are not charged to do beyond your Ability, only to prefer a poor *Brother*, that is a *good Man* and *true*, before any other poor People in the same Circumstances.

Finally, All these *Charges* you are to observe, and also those that shall be communicated to you in *another Way*; cultivating *Brotherly-Love*, the Foundation and Cape-stone, the *Cement* and *Glory* of this antient *Fraternity*, avoiding all Wrangling and Quarrelling, all Slander and Backbiting, nor permitting others to slander any honest Brother, but defending his Character, and doing him all good Offices, as far as is consistent with your *Honour* and *Safety*, and no farther. And if any of them do you Injury you must apply to your own or his *Lodge;* and from thence you may appeal to the *Grand-Lodge* at the *Quarterly Communication,* and from thence to the *annual Grand-Lodge,* as has been the antient laudable Conduct of our Fore-fathers in every Nation; never taking a *legal Course,* but when the Case cannot be otherwise decided, and patiently listning to the honest and friendly Advice of Master and Fellows, when they would prevent your going to Law with *Strangers,* or would excite you to put a speedy Period to all *Law-Suits,* that so you may mind the *Affair* of *Masonry* with the more Alacrity and Success; but with respect to *Brothers* or *Fellows* at Law, the Master and Brethren should kindly offer their Mediation, which ought to be thankfully submitted to by the contending Brethren; and if that Submission is impracticable, they must however carry on their *Process,* or *Law-Suit,* without Wrath and Rancor (not in the common way) saying or doing nothing which may hinder *Brotherly Love,* and good Offices to be renew'd and continu'd; that all may see the *benign Influence* of *Masonry,* as all true *Masons* have done from the Beginning of the *World,* and will do to the End of *Time.*

Amen so mote it be.

General Regulations *for the Use of the* Lodges, *in and about* Dublin; *and approv'd by the* Grand Lodge.

I. THE *Grand-Master* or his *Deputy,* hath Authority and Right, not only to be present in any true *Lodge,* but also to preside wherever he is, with the Master of the *Lodge* on his Left-hand, and to order his Grand-Wardens to attend him, who are not to act in particular Lodges as Wardens, but in his Presence, and at his Command; because there the *Grand-Master* may command the Wardens of that Lodge, or any other Brethrens he pleaseth, to attend and act as his Wardens *pro tempore.*

II. The Master of a particular Lodge has the Right and Authority of congregating the Members of his Lodge into a Chapter at Pleasure, upon any Emergency or Occurrence, as well as to appoint the Time and Place of their usual forming: And in Case of Sickness, Death, or necessary Absence of the Master, the senior Warden shall act as Master *pro tempore*, if no Brother is present who has been Master of that Lodge before; for in that Case the absent Master's Authority reverts to the last Master then present; tho' he cannot act until the said senior Warden has once congregated the Lodge, or in his Absence the junior Warden.

III. The Master of each particular Lodge, or one of the Wardens, or some other Brother by his Order, shall keep a Book containing their *By-Laws*, the Names of their Members, with a List of all the Lodges in Town, and the usual Times and Places of their forming, and all their Transactions that are proper to be written.

IV. No Lodge shall make more than *Five new Brethren* at one Time, nor any Man under the Age of *Twenty-one*, who must be also his own Master; unless by a Dispensation from the *Grand-Master* or his *Deputy*.

V. No Man can be made or admitted a Member of a particular Lodge, without previous notice given to the said Lodge, in order to make due Enquiry into the Reputation and Capacity of the *Candidate*; unless by the Dispensation aforesaid.

VI. But no Man can be entered a *Brother* in any particular Lodge, or admitted to be a Member thereof, without the *unanimous Consent of all the Members of that Lodge* then present when the *Candidate* is propos'd, and their Consent is formally ask'd by the Master; and they are to signify their *Consent* or *Dissent* in their own prudent Way, either virtually or in form, but with Unanimity: Nor is this inherent Privilege subject to a Dispensation, because the Members of a particular Lodge are the best Judges of it; and if a fractious Member should be imposed on them, it might spoil their Harmony, or hinder their Freedom; or even break and disperse the Lodge; which ought to be avoided by all good and true Brethren.

VII. Every *new Brother* at his making is decently to cloath the Lodge, that is, all the Brethren present, and to deposite something for the Relief of indigent and decay'd Brethren, as the *Candidate* shall think fit to bestow, over and above the small Allowance stated by the *By-Laws* of that particular Lodge; which *Charity* shall be lodged with the Master or Wardens, or the Cashier, if the Members think fit to chuse one.

And the *Candidate* shall also solemnly promise to submit to the *Constitutions*, the *Charges*, and *Regulations*, and to such other good *Usages* as shall be intimated to them in Time and Place convenient.

VIII. No set or Number of Brethren shall withdraw or separate themselves from the Lodge in which they were made *Brethren*, or were afterwards admitted Members, unless the Lodge become too numerous; nor even then, without a Dispensation from the *Grand-Master* or his *Deputy*: And when they are thus separated, they must either immediately join themselves to such other Lodge as they shall like best, with the unanimous Consent of that other Lodge to which they go (as *above regulated*) or else they must obtain the *Grand-Master's* Warrant to join in forming a new Lodge.

If any Set or Number of Masons shall take upon themselves to form a Lodge without the *Grand-Master's* Warrant, the regular Lodges are not to countenance them, nor own them as fair *Brethren* and duly form'd, nor approve of their Acts and Deeds; but must treat them as *Rebels*, until they humble themselves, as the *Grand-Master* shall in his Prudence direct, and until he approve of them by his *Warrant*, which must be signified to the other Lodges, as the Costom is when a new Lodge is to be register'd in the List of Lodges.

IX. But if any *Brother* so far misbehave himself as to render his Lodge uneasy, he shall be twice duly admonish'd by the Master or Wardens in a form'd Lodge, and if he will not refrain his Imprudence, and obediently submit to the Advice of the *Brethren*, and reform what gives them Offence, he shall be dealt with according to the *By-Laws* of that particular Lodge, or else in such a Manner as the *Quarterly Communication* shall in their great Prudence think fit.

X. The Majority of every particular Lodge, when congregated, shall have the Privilege of giving *Instructions* to their Master and Wardens, before the assembling of the *Grand Chapter*, or *Lodge*; at the three *Quarterly Communications* hereafter mentioned, and of the *Annual Grand Lodge* too; because their Master and Wardens are their Representatives, and are supposed to speak their Mind.

XI. All particular Lodges are to observe the same *Usages* as much as possible; in order to which, and for cultivating a good Understanding among *Free-Masons*, some Members out of every

Lodge shall be deputed to visit the other Lodges as often as shall be thought convenient.

Of the Grand Lodge.

XII. The *Grand Lodge* consists of, and is form'd by the Masters and Wardens of all the regular particular Lodges upon Record, with the *Grand-Master* at their Head, and his Deputy on his Left-hand, and the Grand-Wardens in their proper Places; and must have a *Quarterly Communication* about *Michaelmas, Christmas,* and *Lady-Day,* in some convenient Place, as the Grand-Master shall appoint, where no *Brother* shall be present, who is not at that time a Member thereof, without a Dispensation; and while he stays, he shall not be allowed to vote, nor even give his Opinion, without leave of the *Grand Lodge* ask'd and given, or unless it be duly ask'd by the said Lodge.

All Matters are to be determined in the *Grand-Lodge* by a Majority of Votes, each Member having one Vote, and the Grand-Master having two Votes, unless the said Lodge leave any particular thing to the Determination of the Grand-Master, for the sake of Expedition.

XIII. At the said *Quarterly Communication*, all Matters that concern the *Fraternity* in general, or particular Lodges, or single Brethren, are quietly, sedately, and maturely to be discours'd of and transacted. Here also all Differences, that cannot be made up and accommodated privately, nor by a particular Lodge, are to be seriously considered and decided: And if any *Brother* thinks himself aggrieved by the Decision of this Board, he may appeal to the *Annual Grand-Lodge* next ensuing, and leave his Appeal in Writing, with the Grand-Master, or his Deputy, or the Grand-Wardens.

Here also the Master or the Wardens of each particular Lodge shall bring and produce a List of such Members as have been made, or even admitted in their particular Lodges since the last *Communication* of the *Grand-Lodge*: And there shall be Book kept by the Grand-Master, or his Deputy, or rather by some *Brother* whom the *Grand-Lodge* shall appoint for *Secretary*, wherein shall be recorded all the Lodges, with their usual Times and Places of forming, and the Names of all the Members of each Lodge; and all the Affairs of the Grand-Lodge that are proper to be written.

They shall also consider of the most prudent and effectual Methods of collecting and disposing of what Money shall be given to, or lodged with them in *Charity*, towards the Relief only of any true *Brother* fallen into Poverty or Decay, but of none else: But every particular Lodge shall dispose of their own *Charity* for poor *Brethren*, according to their own *By-Laws*, until it be agreed by all the Lodges (*in a new Regulation*) to carry in the Charity collected by them to the *Grand-Lodge*, at the *Quarterly* or *Annual Communication*, in order to make a common Stock of it for the more handsome Relief of *poor Brethren*.

They shall also appoint a *Treasurer*, a *Brother* of good worldly Substance, who shall be a Member of the *Grand-Lodge* by vertue of his Office, and shall be always present, and have Power to move to the *Grand-Lodge* any thing, especially what concerns his Office. To him shall be committed all Money rais'd for *Charity*, or for any other Use of the *Grand-Lodge*, which he shall write down in a Book, with the respective Ends and Uses for which the several Sums are intended; and shall expend or disburse the same by such a *certain Order* sign'd, as the *Grand-Lodge* shall agree to: But he shall not vote in chusing a Grand-Master or Wardens, tho' in every other Transaction. As in like manner the *Secretary* shall be a Member of the *Grand-Lodge* by vertue of his Office, and vote in every thing except in chusing a Grand-Master or Wardens.

The *Treasurer* and *Secretary* may have each a Clerk, who must be a *Brother* and Fellow-Craft, but never must be a Member of the *Grand-Lodge*, nor speak without being allowed or desired.

The Grand-Master or his Deputy, shall always command the *Treasurer* and *Secretary*, with their *Clerks* and *Books*, in order to see how Matters go on, and to know what is expedient to be done upon any emergent occasion.

Another *Brother* (who must be a Fellow-Craft) should be appointed to look after the Door of the *Grand-Lodge*; but shall be no Member of it.

XIV. If at any *Grand-Lodge*, stated or occasional, quarterly or annual, the Grand-Master and his Deputy should be both absent, then the present Master of a Lodge, that has been the longest a *Free-Mason*, shall take the Chair, and preside as Grand-Master *pro tempore*; and shall be vested with all his Power and Honour for the time; provided there is no *Brother* present that has been Grand-Master formerly or Deputy Grand Master; for the last Grand-Master present, or else the last Deputy present, should always of right take place in the Absence of the present Grand-Master and his Deputy.

XV. In the *Grand-Lodge* none can act as Wardens but the Grand-Wardens themselves, if present; and if absent, the Grand-Master, or the Person who presides in his Place, shall order private Wardens to act as Grand Wardens *pro tempore*, whose Places are to be supply'd by two Fellow-Crafts of the same Lodge, call'd forth to act, or sent thither by the particlar Master thereof; or if by him omitted, then they shall be call'd by the Grand-Master, that so the *Grand-Lodge* may be always complete.

XVI. The Grand-Wardens, or any others, are first to advise with the Deputy about the Affairs of the Lodge or of the *Brethren*, and not to apply to the Grand-Master without the Knowledge of the Deputy, unless he refuse his Concurrence in any certain necessary Affair; in which Case, or in case of any Difference between the Deputy and the Grand-Wardens, or other *Brethren*, both Parties are to go by Concert to the Grand-Master who can easily decide the Controversy, and make up the Difference by vertue of his great Authority.

The Grand-Master should receive no Intimation of Business concerning MASONRY, but from his Deputy first, except in such certain Cases as his Worship can well judge of; for if the Application to the Grand-Master be irregular, he can easily order the Grand-Wardens, or any other *Brethren* thus applying, to wait upon his Deputy, who is to prepare the Business speedily, and to lay it orderly before his *Worship*.

XVII. No Grand-Master, Deputy Grand-Master, Grand-Wardens, Treasurer, Secretary, or whoever acts for them, or in their stead *pro tempore*, can at the same time be the Master or Warden of a particular Lodge; but as soon as any of them has honourably discharged his *Grand Office*, he returns to that Post or Station in his particular Lodge, from which he was call'd to officiate above.

XVIII. If the *Deputy Grand-Master* be sick, or necessarily absent, the *Grand-Master* may chuse any Fellow-Craft he pleases to be his *Deputy pro tempore*. But he that is chosen *Deputy* at the

Grand-Lodge, and the *Grand-Wardens* too, cannot be discharged without the Cause fairly appear to the Majority of the *Grand-Lodge*; and the *Grand-Master*, if he is uneasy, may call a *Grand-Lodge* on purpose to lay the Cause before them, and to have their Advice and Concurrence: In which case, the Majority of the *Grand-Lodge*, if they cannot reconcile the *Master* and his *Deputy* or his *Wardens*, are to concur in allowing the Master to discharge his said *Deputy* or his said *Wardens*, and to chuse another *Deputy* immediately and the said *Grand-Lodge* shall chuse other *Wardens* in that Case, that Harmony and Peace be preserved.

XIX. If the *Grand-Master* should abuse his Power and render himself unworthy of the Obedience and Subjection of the Lodges; he shall be treated in a way and manner to be agreed upon in a *new Regulation*; because hitherto the antient *Fraternity* have had no occasion for it, their former *Grand-Masters* having all behaved themselves worthy of that honourable Office.

XX. The *Grand-Master*, with *Deputy* and *Wardens*, shall (at least once) go round and visit all the Lodges about Town during his Mastership.

XXI. If the *Grand-Master* die during his Mastership, or by Sickness, or by being beyond Sea, or any other way should be rendered uncapable of discharging his Office, the Deputy, or in his Absence the Senior *Grand-Warden*, or in his Absence the Junior, or in his Absence any three present Masters of Lodges, shall join to congregate the *Grand-Lodge* immediately, to advise together upon that Emergency, and to send two of their Number to invite the last *Grand-Master* to resume his Office, which now in course reverts to him; or if he refuse, then the next last, and so backward: But if no former *Grand-Master* can be found, then the Deputy shall act as *Principal*, until another is chosen; or if there be no Deputy, then the oldest Master.

XXII. The *Brethren* of all the Lodges in and about the City of *Dublin*, shall meet at an *Annual Communication* and *Feast*, in some convenient Place, on *St. John Baptist's Day*, or else on *St. John Evangelist's Day*, as the *Grand-Lodge* shall think fit: Provided,

The Majority of the Masters and Wardens, with the *Grand-Master*, his *Deputy* and *Wardens*, agree at their *Quarterly Communication*, three Months before, that there shall be a *Feast*, and a *General Communication* of all the *Brethren:* For if either the *Grand-Master,* or the Majority of the particular Masters are against it, it must be dropt for that Time.

But whether there shall be a Feast for all the *Brethren,* or not, yet the *Grand-Lodge* must meet in some convenient Place *annually* on *St. John's Day*; or if it be *Sunday,* then on the next Day, in order to chuse every Year a new *Grand-Master, Deputy* and *Wardens.*

XXIII. If it be thought expedient, and the *Grand-Master,* with the Majority of the Masters and Wardens, agree to hold a *Grand-Feast,* according to the antient laudable Customs of *Masons,* then the *Grand-Wardens* shall have the care of preparing the *Tickets,* sealed with the *Grand-Master's* Seal, of disposing of the *Tickets,* of buying the Materials of the *Feast,* of finding out a proper or convenient Place to feast in; and of every other thing that concerns the Entertainment.

But that the Work may not be too burthensome to the two *Grand-Wardens,* and that all Matters may be expeditiously and safely managed, the *Grand-Master,* or his *Deputy,* shall have Power to nominate and appoint a certain Number of *Stewards,* as his *Worship* shall think fit, to act in concert with the two *Grand-Wardens*; all things relating to the *Feast* being decided amongst them by a Majority of Voices; except the *Grand-Master* or his *Deputy* interpose by a particular Direction or Appointment.

XXIV. The *Wardens* and *Stewards* shall, in due time, wait upon the *Grand-Master,* or his *Deputy,* for Directions and Orders about the Premises; but if his *Worship* and his *Deputy* are sick, or necessarily absent, they shall call together the Masters and Wardens of Lodges to meet on purpose for their Advice and Orders; or else they may take the Matter wholly upon themselves, and do the best they can.

The *Grand-Wardens* and the *Stewards* are to account for all the Money they receive, or expend, to the *Grand-Lodge,* after Dinner, or when the *Grand-Lodge* shall think fit to receive their Accounts.

If the *Grand-Master* pleases, he may in due time summon all the Masters and Wardens of Lodges to consult with them about ordering the *Grand-Feast,* and about any Emergency or accidental thing relating thereunto, that may require Advice; or else to take it upon himself altogether.

XXV. The *Masters of Lodges* shall appoint one experienced and discreet Fellow-Craft of his Lodge, to compose a Committee, consisting of one from every Lodge, who shall meet to receive, in a convenient Apartment, every Person that brings a Ticket, and shall have Power to discourse him, if they think fit, in order to admit him, or debar him, as they shall see cause: Provided they send no Man away before they have acquainted all the Brethren within Doors with the Reasons thereof, to avoid Mistakes; that so no true Brother may be debarred, nor a false Brother or mere Pretender, admitted. This *Committee* must meet very early on *St. John's Day* at the Place, even before any Persons come with Tickets.

XXVI. The *Grand-Master* shall appoint two or more *trusty Brethren* to be Porters, or Door-keepers, who are also to be early at the Place, for some good Reasons; and who are to be at the Command of the *Committee*.

XXVII. The *Grand-Wardens*, or the *Stewards*, shall appoint beforehand such a Number of *Brethren* to serve at Table as they think fit and proper for that Work; and they may advise with the Masters and Wardens of Lodges about the most proper Persons, if they please, or may take in such by their Recommendation; for none are to serve that Day, but *free and accepted Masons*, that the Communication may be free and harmonious.

XXVIII. All the Members of the *Grand-Lodge* must be at the Place long before Dinner, with the *Grand-Master*, or his *Deputy*, at their Head, who shall retire, and form themselves. And this is done in order,

1. To receive any *Appeals* duly lodg'd, as above regulated, that the *Appellant* may be heard, and the Affair may be amicably decided before Dinner, if possible; but if it cannot, it must be delayed till after the *new Grand-Master* is elected; and if it cannot be decided after Dinner, it may be delayed, and referr'd to a *particular Committee*, that shall quietly adjust it, and make Report to the next *Quarterly Communication*, that Brotherly-Love may be preserved.

2. To prevent any Difference or Disgust which may be feared

to arise that Day; that no Interruption may be given to the Harmony and Pleasure of the *Grand-Feast*.

3. To consult about whatever concerns the Decency and Decorum of the *Grand-Assembly*, and to prevent all Indecency and ill Manners, the Assembly being promiscuous.

4. To receive and consider of any good Motion, or any momentous and important Affair, that shall be brought from the particular Lodges, by their Representatives, the several *Masters* and *Wardens*.

XXIX. After these things are discuss'd, the *Grand-Master* and his *Deputy*, the *Grand-Wardens*, or the *Stewards*, the *Secretary*, the *Treasurer*, the *Clerks*, and every other Person, shall withdraw, and leave the Masters and Wardens of the particular Lodges alone, in order to consult amicably about electing a *New Grand-Master*, or continuing the *present*, if they have not done it the Day before; and if they are unanimous for continuing the *present* Grand-Master, his *Worship* shall be call'd in, and humbly desired to do the *Fraternity* the Honour of ruling them for the Year ensuing: And after Dinner it will be known whether he accepts of it or not: For it should not be discovered but by the Election itself.

XXX. Then the Masters and Wardens, and all the *Brethren*, may converse promiscuously, or as they please to sort together, until the Dinner is coming in, when every *Brother* takes his Seat at Table.

XXXI. Some time after Dinner the *Grand-Lodge* is form'd, not in Retirement, but in the Presence of all the *Brethren*, who yet are not Members of it, and must not, therefore, speak until they are desired and allowed.

XXXII. If the *Grand-Master* of last Year has consented with the Master and Wardens in private, before Dinner, to continue for the Year ensuing; then *one* of the *Grand-Lodge*, deputed for that purpose, *shall represent to all the Brethren his* Worship's *good Government*, &c. And turning to him, shall, in the Name of the *Grand-Lodge*, humbly request him to do the *Fraternity the great Honour* (if nobly born, if not) *the great Kindness* of continuing to be their *Grand-Master* for the Year ensuing. And his *Worship* declaring his Consent by a Bow or a Speech, as he pleases, the said *deputed Member* of the *Grand-Lodge* shall proclaim him

Grand-Master, and all the Members of the *Lodge* shall salute him in Due Form. And all the *Brethren* shall for a few Minutes have leave to declare their satisfaction, Pleasure, and Congratulation.

XXXIII. But if either the Master and Wardens have not in private, this Day before Dinner, nor the Day before, desired the last *Grand-Master* to continue in the *Mastership* another Year; or, if he, when desired, has not consented: Then,

The last *Grand-Master* shall nominate his Successor for the Year ensuing, who, if unanimously approv'd by the *Grand-Lodge*, and if there present, shall be proclaimed, saluted, and congratulated the *New Grand-Master* as above hinted, and immediately installed by the last Grand-Master, according to Usage.

XXXIV. But if that Nomination is not unanimously approv'd, the new Grand-Master shall be chosen immediately by *Ballot*, every Master and Warden writing his Man's Name, and the last Grand-Master writing his Man's Name too; and the Man, whose Name the last Grand Master shall first take out, carefully or by chance, shall be *Grand Master* for the Year ensuing; and if present, he shall be proclaimed, saluted, and congratulated, as above hinted, and forthwith installed by the last Grand-Master, according to Usage.

XXXV. The last Grand Master thus continued, or the new Grand-Master thus install'd, shall next nominate and appoint his Deputy *Grand-Master*, either the last or a new one, who shall be also declared, saluted and congratulated as above hinted.

The *Grand-Master* shall also nominate the *new Grand-Wardens*, and if unanimously approved by the *Grand-Lodge*, shall be declared, saluted, and congratulated, as above hinted; but if not, they shall be chosen by *Ballot*, in the same way as the *Grand-Master*: As the Wardens of private Lodges are also to be chosen by *Ballot* in each Lodge, if the Members thereof do not agree to the Master's Nomination.

XXXVI. But if the *Brother*, whom the present *Grand-Master* shall nominate for his *Successor*, or whom the Majority of the *Grand-Lodge* shall happen to chuse by *Ballot*, is by Sickness or other necessary Occasion, absent from the *Grand-Feast*, he cannot be proclaim'd the new *Grand-Master*, unless the old *Grand-Master*, or some of the *Masters* and *Wardens* of the *Grand-Lodge* can vouch, upon the *Honour* of a *Brother*, that the said Person, so nominated or chosen, will readily accept the said Office; in which Case the old *Grand Master* shall act as Proxy, and shall nominate the Deputy and Wardens in his Name, and in his Name also receive the usual Honours, Homage, and Congratulation.

XXXVII. Then the *Grand Master* shall allow any *Brother, Fellow-Craft,* or *Apprentice* to speak, directing his Discourse to his *Worship*; or to make any Motion for the good of the *Fraternity,* which shall be either immediately considered and finished, or else referred to the Consideration of the *Grand-Lodge,* at their next *Communication,* stated or occasional. When that is over,

XXXVIII. The *Grand Master* or his *Deputy,* or some *Brother* appointed by him, shall harangue all the *Brethren,* and give them good Advice: And, lastly, after some other Transactions, that cannot be written in any Language, the *Brethren* may go away or stay longer, as they please.

XXXIX. Every *Annual Grand Lodge* has an inherent Power and Authority to make *new Regulations,* or to alter these, for the real Benefit of this *antient Fraternity*: Provided always, that the old Land-Marks *be carefully preserved,* and that such Alterations and *new* Regulations be proposed and agreed to at the third *Quarterly Communication* preceding the *Annual Grand Feast*; and that they be offered also to the Perusal of all the *Brethren* before Dinner, in Writing, even of the youngest *Apprentice*; the Approbation and Consent of the Majority of all the *Brethren* present being absolutely necessary to make the same binding and obligatory; which must, after Dinner, and after the new *Grand Master* is installed, be solemnly desired; as it was desired and obtained for these *Regulations,* when proposed by the *Grand Lodge.*

The Manner of constituting a NEW LODGE, *according to the antient Usage of* MASONS.

A *New Lodge,* for avoiding many Irregularities, should be solemnly constituted by the *Grand Master,* with his Deputy and Wardens; or in the *Grand Master's* Absence, the Deputy shall act for his *Worship,* and shall chuse some Master of a Lodge to assist him; or in case the Deputy is absent, the *Grand Master* shall call forth some Master of a Lodge to act as Deputy *pro tempore.*

The *Candidates*, or the new Master and Wardens, being yet among the *Fellow-Craft*, the *Grand Master* shall ask his Deputy if he has examined them, and finds the Candidate Master well skill'd in the *noble Science* and the *Royal Art*, and duly instructed in our *Mysteries*, &c.

And the Deputy answering in the Affirmative, he shall (by the *Grand Master's* Order) take the *Candidate* from among his Fellows, and present him to the Grand Master; saying, *Right Worshipful* Grand Master, *the Brethren here desire to be formed into a* new Lodge; *and I present this my worthy* Brother *to be their* Master, *whom I know to be of good Morals and great Skill, true and trusty, and a lover of the whole* Fraternity, *wheresoever dispersed over the face of the* Earth.

Then the Grand Master placing the *Candidate* on his left Hand, having ask'd and obtained the unanimous consent of all the Brethren, shall say, *I constitute and form these good* Brethren *into a* new Lodge, *and appoint you the* Master *of it, not doubting of your Capacity and Care to preserve the* Cement *of the* Lodges, *&c.* with some other Expressions that are proper and usual on that Occasion, but not proper to be written.

Upon this the Deputy shall rehearse the *Charges* of a Master, and the Grand Master shall ask the *Candidate*, saying, *Do you submit to these* Charges, *as* Masters *have done in all Ages?* And the *Candidate* signifying his cordial Submission thereunto, the Grand Master shall, by certain significant Ceremonies and antient Usages, install him, and present him with the *Constitutions*, the *Lodge Book*, and the *Instruments* of his Office, not all together, but one after another; and after each of them, the Grand Master, or his Deputy, shall rehearse the short and pithy *Charge* that is suitable to the Thing presented.

After this, the Members of this new Lodge, bowing all together to the Grand Master, shall return his *Worship* Thanks, and immediately do their *Homage* to their *new Master*, and signify their Promise of Subjection and Obedience to him by the usual *Congratulation*.

The Deputy and the Grand Wardens, and any other Brethren present, that are not Members of this new Lodge, shall next congratulate the new *Master*; and he shall return his becoming Acknowledgments to the Grand Master first, and to the rest in their order.

Then the Grand Master desires the new *Master* to enter immediately upon the Exercise of his Office, in chusing his Wardens: And the new *Master* calling forth two *Fellow-Craft*, presents them to the *Grand Master* for his Approbation, and to the new Lodge for their Consent. And that being granted,

The senior or junior Grand Warden, or some Brother for him, shall rehearse the *Charges* of Wardens; and the *Candidates* being solemnly ask'd by the new *Master*, shall signify their Submission thereunto.

Upon which the new Master, presenting them with the *Instruments* of their Office, shall, in due Form, install them in their proper Places; and the Brethren of that new Lodge shall signify their Obedience to the new Wardens by the usual *Congratulation*.

> And this Lodge being thus compleatly constituted, shall be register'd in the *Grand-Master's* Book, and by his Order notify'd to the other Lodges.

A Short CHARGE *to be given to new admitted* BRETHREN.

YOU are now admitted by the unanimous Consent of our Lodge, a *Fellow* of our most Antient and Honourable *Society*; *Antient*, as having subsisted from Times immemorial, and *Honourable*, as tending in every particular to render a Man so that will be but conformable to its glorious Precepts. The greatest Monarchs in all Ages, as well as *Asia* and *Africa* as of *Europe*, have been Encouragers of the *Royal Art*; and many of them have presided as *Grand-Masters* over the *Masons* in their respective Territories, not thinking it any lessening to their Imperial Dignities to level themselves with their *Brethren* in MASONRY, and to act as they did.

The World's great *Architect* is our *Supreme Master*, and the unerring Rule he has given us, is that by which we Work.

Religious Disputes are never uttered in the Lodge, for as *Masons*, we only pursue the universal Religion of Nature. This is the Cement which unites Men of the most different Principles in one sacred Band, and brings together those who were the most distant from one another.

There are three general Heads of Duty, which MASONS ought always to inculcate, *viz.* to *God,* our *Neighbours,* and *Ourselves.*

To God, in never mentioning his Name but with that Reverential Awe which becomes a Creature to bear to his Creator, and to look upon him always as the *Summum Bonum* which we came into the World to enjoy; and according to that View to regulate all our Pursuits.

To our Neighbours, in acting upon the Square, or doing as we would be done by.

To Ourselves, in avoiding all Intemperances and Excesses, whereby we may be rendered incapable of following our Work, or led into Behaviour unbecoming our laudable Profession, and, in always keeping within due Bounds, and free from all Pollution.

In the State, a MASON is to behave as a peaceable and dutiful Subject, conforming cheerfully to the Government under which he lives.

He is to pay a due Deference to his Superiors, and from his Inferiors he is rather to receive Honour with some Reluctance, than to extort it.

He is to be a Man of Benevolence and Charity, not sitting down contented while his Fellow Creatures, but much more his *Brethren,* are in Want, when it is in his Power (without prejudicing himself or Family) to relieve them.

In the Lodge, he is to behave with all due Decorum, lest the Beauty and Harmony thereof should be disturbed or broke.

He is to be obedient to the Master and presiding Officers, and to apply himself closely to the Business of MASONRY, that he may sooner become a Proficient therein, both for his own Credit, and for that of the Lodge.

He is not to neglect his own necessary Avocations for the sake of MASONRY, nor to involve himself in Quarrels with those who through Ignorance may speak evil of, or ridicule it.

He is to be a Lover of the Arts and Sciences, and to take all Opportunities of improving himself therein.

If he recommends a Friend to be made a *Mason,* he must vouch him to be such as he really believes will conform to the aforesaid Duties, lest by his Misconduct at any Time the Lodge should pass under some evil Imputations. Nothing can prove more shocking to all faithful MASONS, than to see any of their *Brethren* profane or break through the sacred Rules of their Order, and such as can do it they wish had never been admitted.

APPROBATION.

WE the GRAND MASTER of the Right Worshipful and Most Antient *Fraternity* of *Free* and *accepted Masons*, the *Depputy Grand-Master*, and the *Grand-Wardens*, having perused this POCKET-COMPANION, do give our solemn Approbation for the printing the same; and do recommend it for the Use of the *Brethren*.

      KINGSLAND, *Grand Master*.
      JAMES BRENAN, M. D. *Deputy*.
      WM. COBBE,
      JOHN BALDWIN, } *Esqrs*, G.W.

THE MASONIC BOOK CLUB

OFFICERS FOR 1974-77

LOUIS L. WILLIAMS
President
111 Rust Road
Bloomington, Illinois 61701

ALPHONSE CERZA
Secretary
237 Millbridge Road
Riverside, Illinois 60546

FRED A. DOLAN
Vice-President
218 Imperial Drive
Bloomington, Illinois 61701

JAMES H. BICKET
Treasurer
1909 E. Oakland Avenue
Bloomington, Illinois 61701

ADVISORY BOARD

HARRY CARR

J. ALLEN CABANISS

WALTER CALLAWAY, JR.

WILLIAM R. DENSLOW

CHARLES GOSNELL

CONRAD HAHN

DR. EUGENE S. HOPP

LEE LOCKWOOD

DWIGHT L. SMITH

J. FAIRBAIRN SMITH

MEMBERS

UNITED STATES

ALABAMA
Rev. Benjamin F. Atkins
Edmund H. Duffey
John E. Foster
Nichols C. Hobbs
J. W. Hollingsworth
C. V. McLain, Jr.
Lt. Col. H. Edward May
Mobile Lodge of Perfection
Henry Petersen, Jr.
H. Edward Stout

ALASKA
Peter Switzer

ARIZONA
Gerald A. Aaron, Jr.
Robert L. Griffin
Robert L. Haupert
John Keegan
William E. Keegan, Jr.
Charles A. Mattingly
Rev. Donald W. Monson
Dean Tillotson

ARKANSAS
Theodore J. Bailey, Sr.
Jackie Dobson
John H. Green
Clarke J. McLane
William Nash

CALIFORNIA
Milton E. Ammann
Edward E. Anderson
Edwin A. Arnold
Virl Bennehoff
Charles M. Bozza
Joseph Brod
Al Brotherton
Calexico Lodge No. 412
Jess B. Coleman, Jr.
William J. Crawford
Stanley Creelman
Dr. Hector M. de Alva
Nicholas N. Domansky
El Camino Research Lodge
Jerry R. Erikson
Enoch H. Fratis
Fresno Scottish Rite Bodies
Charles Galbraith
Dr. John J. Hancock
Ralph A. Herbold
Dr. Eugene S. Hopp

Myrl W. Hurley
Ted Wallace Ince
James L. Jones
James F. Justice
Daniel S. Kamis
Bobby Kelly
Prescott B. Kinsman
John C. Lake
Dr. Harry C. Layton
Morton D. Leaderman
Chester E. Lee
Victor J. Leonardi
Robert D. Lintner
Allen J. Lockwood
Long Beach Scottish
    Rite Bodies
Howard M. Magill
L. R. Mauro
Robert W. Meier
John R. Nocas
Albert C. O'Connell
Villard J. Paddio
Attilio G. Parisi
Lewis Penn
William F. Poynter
Harold M. Preston
Vernon B. Prink
Clarence Ranslem
Melville Richards
Edwin D. Rogers
Howard E. Rolan
Cecil A. Ryder, Jr.
San Diego Scottish
    Rite Library
Wentworth A. Sankey
Robert H. Siegel
Leo Slevin
Southern California
    Masonic Library
Porter Stanley
Quincy A. Sutton
Otto L. Wheeler
Earl Williams
Richard H. Williamson

COLORADO
Carroll L. Bloom
John P. Burke
William Engelker
D. C. Ingraham
Dr. F. Bing Johnson
Grand Lodge of Colorado
    Library
Gordon R. Merrick
Nevada Lodge No. 4
Scott L. Palmer

Kenneth E. Pool
Carl H. Peterson
Research Lodge of Colorado
Renno S. Shaw
King Wheeler
Kenneth E. Wiese

CONNECTICUT
Raymond H. Dragat
Hames W. Field
Robert Juif
Fred W. Mindermann
Irving E. Partridge

DELAWARE
William H. Cantwell
Robert C. Kersey
Henry G. Law
Harry J. Littleton
Donald D. Thomas

DISTRICT OF COLUMBIA
Library of the Supreme
    Council, 33°

FLORIDA
Frank A. Abrahams
LTC Richard B. Baldwin
James H. Brown
Dekran Dorian
Fred W. Evans
Roland M. Fennimore
Paul G. Hagenbuch
Dr. Paul H. Jahn
Irwin Lechowitz
Joseph H. Moffat
Lloyd W. Owens
Robert E. Prest
Robert L. Schultz
James S. Scofield
Howard M. Smith
Carl E. Strom
Grand W. Walters

GEORGIA
Harris Bullock
Carlton E. Byers
Walter M. Callaway, Jr.
David L. Canaday
Hy Chinkes
Fred H. Crouch, Jr.
William W. Daniel
Donald E. Davis
John A. Dunaway
Louis Elton Durden
R. G. Ebrey
George W. Finger
Dr. William R. Fisher
Earl D. Harris

Julian M. Hodgskin, Jr.
Ralph C. James
David H. Lanier
Masonic Research Lodge No. 104
Clifford M. Merrill
Ogeechee Lodge No. 213
Pembroke Lodge No. 469
Robert S. Porter
Tommy G. Rogers
Robert L. Richards
Lanier F. Rogers
William H. Sachs
Richard S. Sagar
Morris B. Smith, Jr.
Solomon's Lodge No. 1
A. F. Spell
Madison H. Stephen
John M. Stine
James W. Thayer
George E. White
Lee H. Williams
Carl J. Woeltjen

ILLINOIS
Edward R. Ahlenius
William H. Ahlenius
Albert L. Anderson
Raymond H. Bachman
Ray Barnd
William D. Barnes
Albert J. Bell
G. Wilbur Bell
James H. Bicket
Grant D. Biddle
Walter H. Brown
C. K. Brownfield
Norman R. Buecker
George E. Burow
J. Garrie Burr
Charles L. Cannon
Chalmers E. Carroll
P. Mason Carruthers
Robert E. Clark
Alphonse Cerza
Harry X. Cole
Hugh A. Cole
Jean E. Cranston
Alvin L. Crump
Danville Scottish
    Rite Bodies
Hubert C. Davis
Milton D. Dirst
Fred A. Dolan, Jr.
Charles C. Figeley
C. Wayne Franklin
Charles F. Gambill
Carl L. Gardner
Garnett S. Todd, Jr.
William D. Gilstrap

Glenview Lodge No. 1058
Richard A. Greig
Wayne H. Harper
John W. Heafer, Sr.
Orval J. Hiscox
Bruce D. Hudson
Stephan Huziany
Dr. Ridell A. Kelsey
Harold O. Klein
Harold R. Kopfman
Charles Kouba
Henry H. Kramer
David L. Laske
W. John Leary
Wolcott N. Lyon, Jr.
Louis R. McDonald
Raymond B. McNattin
Donald E. Meseth
John T. Neeley
Allan D. Parsons
Robert L. Pemberton
Wayne A. Petersen
Leon Postlewait
George C. Prager
Kurth Raillard
David M. Reinhardt
Carl L. Rhodes
Harold L. Richmond
Aitken Riddle
Raymond M. Ring
Thomas C. Roberts
Paul C. Rodenhauser
Warren J. Rodrian
Craig L. Rohrer
Elmer Gene Ross
Edmund R. Sadowski
George W. Schabow
Glenn C. Schmeltzer
Martin W. Schuele
Scottish Rite Bodies,
    Freeport, Ill.
Robert B. Skipton
Chester B. Steele
Dean V. Stelle
Paul R. Stephens
J. R. Stockner
George C. Storm, Jr.
Peter J. Tatooles
John M. Thompson
Earl F. Torell
Andrew N. Torok
Oswell G. Treadway
William D. Tucker
Don R. Ulrey
Michael P. Unitson
Irvin A. Uphoff
Valley of Chicago, A.A.S.R.
Vance C. Van Tassell
Louis H. Voss, Sr.
N. Tracy Walker

J. Robert Watt
Arthur A. Webb
Harold Weston
Benjamin C. Willis
Louis D. Williams
Louis L. Williams
Dale C. Wright
Del York
Philip J. Zimmerman, Sr.
Samuel K. Zipp
Albert C. Zrna
Homer L. Zumwalt
James R. DePew

INDIANA
Herbert H. Anderson
Joseph A. Batchelor
Charles R. Brown
Samuel R. Caswell
John Collie, Jr.
Neil L. Crumb
Arnold O. Davis
John H. Double
C. C. Faulkner, Jr.
John W. Fisher
James B. Gale
Grand Lodge of Indiana
Gerald A. Hancock
Robert J. Hepler
Theo John Jena
Robert P. Joyce
Ted E. Kaptain
Theodore H. Kittell
Carl B. Leslie
Kurt Marx
Donald H. Miller
Robert D. Montgomery
Doyle W. Oursler
Dr. D. R. Reed
Dr. Robert M. Seibel
Dwight L. Smith
Ronald K. Smith
Kenneth W. Toler
Lewis B. Travioli
Joseph Triolo
Harrison B. Williams
Donald E. Woodling

IDAHO
Dale N. LeMaire

IOWA
Thomas D. Bachtell
George C. Campbell
Doyle Champion
Charles W. Delk
Allen Heaton
Robert M. Hoverton
Iowa Masonic Library
Howard L. Knupp

Willis F. Lathrop
Leonard W. Lotts
Jerold E. Marsengill
John B. Sheeler
Robert L. Smith
John Harris Watts

KANSAS
John F. Bohm
S. Allan Daugherty
Thomas L. Francis
James L. Kusnerus
Alfred L. Lewis
Masonic Bodies of Emporia
Nelse K. Nelson
Roger Smith
Robert H. Stevens

KENTUCKY
Z'Thomas K. Cannon
Charles S. Guthrie, Jr.
Charles K.A. McGaughey
Horace Glenn Ray
R. O. Smith
Rodney Williams, Sr.

LOUISIANA
Sylvester M. Arnold
Donald P. Boaz
Donald M. Cameron
Bruce D. Christensen
Dr. Hollis U. Cox
Dwight A. Dahmes
John G. Keretz
Merritt S. Pilcher IV
Abraham W. Roy, Jr.
Marvin K. Sloan
Ballard L. Smith
Allen E. Stephens

MAINE
Bruce A. Allen
Camille L. Bolduc
Charles R. Glassmire
Grand Lodge of Maine
Dr. Loring W. Pratt
Richard L. Rhoda
Donald S. Smith
Norman L. Thing
Philip D. Tingley
Robert E. Wilson

MINNESOTA
Jon K. Allsen
Charles E. Boughton
Walter A. Ferrell
William J. Hepler
John Hallberg Jones
Jerry R. Korstad

Harry P. Larson
Ronald J. Nordin
Julius W. Opheim
Everett Schwoch
Fred J. Williams

MARYLAND
Carroll W. Bowman
Dr. Samuel Dubin
Edgar Lars Gresham
Conrad Hahn
Dr. Grant L. Hagen
Walter L. Hagen
George H. Hocker
Lenwood L. Jenkins
Thaddeus Perry
Aemil Pouler
William O. Renner
David L. Rinehart
Herbert E. Stats
Milton R. Wheatley, Sr.

MASSACHUSETTS
Joseph F. Beucler
Dr. Albert L. Biller
Cyril E. Brubaker
David E. Carlson
Lorenzo B. Carr
Robert E. Day
Ralph B. Duncan
Abraham Feldman
Alvah D. Gardiner
Edward W. Gelinas
Grand Lodge of Masons
Mitchell P. Krach
Roopen Manoggian
Robert B. Neff
Rev. Paul J. Rich
Supreme Council, N.M.J.,U.S.A.
Milton M. Tuff
Stephen J. Twining, Sr.
Kenneth E. Vinal

MICHIGAN
Charles K. Bohn
Benjamin J. Brandt
Marvin F. Brown
Robert J. Cameron
Victor Castle, Sr.
Thomas A. Crane
R. E. Curlis
Paul B. Dailey
Richard G. Deane
Orel Du Fresne
Alan Eugene Eichman
Robert D. Hart
Walter Hutchins
Donald G. Ingell
Taisto M. Kataja

Ted Kimball
Frank A. Lane
Donald A. Lenz
Richard Meretsky
Roger W. Morris
Robert L. Murphy
Alan T. Nelson
William E. Parker
Harry Runyon
Richard H. Sands
Erwin A. Salisbury
Gerald E. Sessions
James Fairbairn Smith
Richard M. Strauss
Robert R. Taft
I. Bud Talbot
James E. Vernon
Bernhard W. Vosteen

MISSISSIPPI
William E. Belt
J. Allen Cabaniss
H. N. Eason

MISSOURI
Acacia Lodge No. 602
Franklin J. Anderson
Norman Andonoff
Vernon R. Arms
Leonard V. Bowers
Staton T. Brown
Clarene L. Bush
Bert W. Casselman
W. H. Chapman
Thomas J. Davis, Jr.
Earl K. Dille
Floyd E. Dodson
Harry Gershenson
Prof. Harold O. Brauel
Alfred W. Griffith
Emory J. Hampel
Albert Johnson
Edward McMurry
Clint E. Moffitt
Douglas C. Mornin
Robert F. Pyatt
Royal Arch Magazine
Alfred E. Spencer
John B. Vrooman
Richard Whitney
Charles E. Woodson
David W. Worsdell

MONTANA
Harry Cameron
Francis L. Eukes
George E. Francis
Ludvik H. Jun
Robert H. Klotzman

Glen Raney
James L. Simpson

NEBRASKA
Charles F. Adams
Howard D. Franklin
Lawrence F. Malchow
Lewis R. Ricketts
Louis V. Sylvester
Lawrence J. Zwart

NEVADA
Clark Billingsley
Joseph Bureski
G. William Casteel
Clarence K. Jones
Michael W. Leonard
Victor D. Robison
Silas E. Ross
Kenneth B. Thompson

NEW HAMPSHIRE
Anniversary Lodge of
  Research No. 175
Leonard A. Kangas
North Star Lodge No. 8

NEW JERSEY
Andrew H. Adams
Lewis J. Birt
Frank W. Bobb
Nelson H. Cornell
E. W. Davis
Wallace M. Gage
Joseph R. Gilbert
Daniel W. Hand, Jr.
John T. Koedderich
Edward Lisy
Haydn R. Jones
North Star Lodge No. 255
Donald L. Pellington
William F. Roberts
Scottish Rite Bodies of Trenton
Joseph J. Anthony Suozzi
Denis B. Woodfield

NEW MEXICO
Dr. Sidney Auerbach
Ronald A. Brinkman
Research Lodge of New Mexico
Louis E. Perkal

NEW YORK
Leland H. Benedict
Robert A. L. Bentley
Louis Bernstein
Raymond F. Blomberg
Allan Boudreau
Wilmer E. Bresee

L. Sherman Brooks
Richard H. Brown
Harold J. Cady
Edward C. Coakley
Walter H. Cummings
Aloysius H. Curran
John W. Dellera
Raymond C. Dickieson
Raymond E. Durham, Jr.
Robert E. Freyer
Geneva Masonic Memorial Library
Charles E. Glidewell
Dr. Charles F. Gosnell
Raymond P. Grieb
Leo L. Heneghan
Gordon W. Kent
Robert T. Lambert
Altman W. Lampe
Dr. Oscar A. Lang
Gale W. Lees
Ralph E. Lewis
Melvin H. Levy
Walter J. Maier
Rev. Don C. Markham
Donald F. May
Terry D. McLaughlin
William F. Meehan
Charles L. Morris
George A. Newbury
James L. Nichols, Jr.
Dr. William G. Peacher
Frank E. Philpitt
Frank Polchlopek
Norman D. Powers, Jr.
Charles J. Reilly
Floyd E. Sillaway
Arthur B. Shaw
Robert A. Smith
Major Thomas A. Spencer
Herbert H. Stafford
James A. Stors
Edward R. Troslin, Jr.
John C. Van Gorden
Stanley A. Weeks
Elroy P. Walker
Ronald E. Westman
Dr. Joe R. Willard

NORTH CAROLINA
Robert A. Boggs
Benjamin J. Bulluck, Jr.
Dr. Byron H. Brow, Jr.
Rev. M. L. De Hart
John N. Graeber
Hubert C. Holt
Boyd Hopkins
Otis V. Jones, Jr.
William K. Lonsdale
Dr. Craig R. MacClean

Terry W. McCammon
Gerald W. Ringler
John L. Stickley
Dr. Eddie P. Stiles

NORTH DAKOTA
William J. Brooks
Edward J. Franta
Stephen D. Hodges
Fred J. Nehrenberg
Ernest R. Nyman
Forrest S. Sharkey
Dr. A. J. Springan

OHIO
William D. Beers
Jack D. Brammer
Sydney G. Brooks
Glenn G. Buirley
John A. Busic
Harry H. Cole
Frank Duman
Edward A. Forshaw
Franklin G. Gepfert
Lewis Hoffman
Richard M. Holz
Ernest C. Kegley
John A. Lloyd
Meyer W. Minkin
Carl A. Nissen, Jr.
Paul Nyitray
Lewis Richter
Ellsworth C. Rife
Richard J. Runyon
Royal C. Scofield
Richard L. Speer
Wayne E. Stichter
Donald L. Stupp
Herbert S. Taylor
The Masonic Library Asso.
   of Cincinnati
Harold M. Thomas
Floyd P. Tye
James M. Vieth
William Wadl
Herbert N. Weaver
Karl Weick
Western Star Lodge No. 21
Edgar R. Wightman
Stanley C. Wyllie

OKLAHOMA
Bartlesville Lodge No. 284
Bill Becquart
Edgar O. Fox
J. Fred Latham
Joseph S. Lewis
Bernard F. Mandelbaum
Charles P. Rosenberger

William Howard Wheat

OREGON
Daniel B. Baptist
Walter K. Belt
Bliss O. Bignall
Grand Lodge of Oregon
Wilbur G. Jenkins
Earl H. Reynolds
W. Walter Stuart, Jr.
James Westerfield

PENNSYLVANIA
Nelson M. Baird, Jr.
Raymond D. Beaver
Arthur B. Besnecker
Errol T. Betzenberger
Robert E. Daume, Jr.
Paul E. Davidheiser
Robert L. Engel
Thomas C. Espieg
Paul D. Fisher
Edward H. Fowler
Ralph C. Frantz
Vincent C. Fry
Joseph Gentile
Paul T. Goebig
Robert W. Hassell
Lawrence Hay
Elwood R. Hebbe, Jr.
Earl Heffner
Francis D. Hoffstot
Edward L. Helgerman
Benjamin A. Isaacson
John W. Kloss
Library, Grand Lodge
   of Pennsylvania
John Losten
Robert H. Mason
Spencer C. Masters
W. J. McCulley, Jr.
Bertram Messerly
George F. Miller
Robert D. Miller
Davis S. Nagle
Kenneth W. Nebinger
George A. Neiffer
Donald S. Oplinger
Norman H. Pracht
Vernon E. Quay
John H. Rickert
Harry H. Ritts, Jr.
Robert C. Roberts
Robert L. Sadler
J. Weaver Sames
Victor L. Schumacher
Dr. Whitlaw M. Show
Edgar R. Sims, Jr.
William S. Solliday
Floyd R. Sowers

R. Casper Swaney
Willis G. Thomas, Jr.
Robert K. Toward
Albert E. Turner, III
Mont C. Welch
Gerald W. West
Fred L. Williams, III
Donald Francis Young
Charles E. Zarfos
Earl A. Zimber

RHODE ISLAND
Norris G. Abbott, Jr.
Harold W. Higley
Donald A. Kemp
Harry T. Madeira
Temple Lodge Library

SOUTH CAROLINA
John J. Brewington
Daniel F. Dukes, Jr.
Wallace F. Kuhner
Ralph M. Magoffin
Dr. Basil Manly, IV
William E. Payne
George W. Suttle
Louis O. Tibbs
Thomas Harry White
William V. Wilson

SOUTH DAKOTA
Grand Lodge of South Dakota
Charles F. Parks
Rev. George R. Stracke
Harold L. Tisher

TENNESSEE
Joe R. Coker
O. Earl Cook, Jr.
Harold Cristil
Yeaman Bennett
Charles W. Davis
Roger J. Donovan
Hurley Goforth, Jr.
John F. Kelly, Jr.
John W. Knox
Robert A. Mann
Dr. Robert A. McCrummen
William H. McGinnis, Jr.
Dr. William K. Owen
W. B. Quillen, III
Jethro D. Tisdale
James P. Wagner
James T. Williams
John W. Williams
Howard E. Wolery
E. O. Wynne

TEXAS
H. C. Arbuckle, III
Joe W. Clark
Carroll C. Coker
Roger W. Coltey
Paul E. Cox
H. Proctor Crow, Jr.
Robert L. Dillard, Jr.
Leonard M. Ellington
Kenneth C. England
Leonard L. Fitzgerald
Dr. George H. T. French
Alton L. Garrett
Kenneth D. Gemmell
Will Port Hall
Herbert L. Halladay
Frank D. Hensel
Dr. Robert H. Hutchinson
Naren L. Jackson
Ward C. Johnson, Jr.
Dan Kamp
A. R. Langston
Royce P. Larned
James H. Lewis
Col. William D. Lewis
Lee Lockwood
George S. Mann
Thomas D. Murphy, Jr.
Douglas Peveto
Joe W. Regian
Leonard Resnick
Lenville Rogers
Robert L. Roseberry
Texas Grand Lodge Library
James K. Todd, Jr.
Plez A. Transou
Ben Wilson, Jr.
C. Danny Wilson
Hurley G. Work

UTAH
Mervin B. Hogan
Loran D. Koon
William G. Lapsley
Charles A. McGee

VERMONT
Dr. Frank H. Caffin, Jr.
Norman B. Kewley
Charles R. Pierce

VIRGINIA
Samuel T. Atkinson
Martin K. Brooks
William E. Copenhaver
James F. Florance
Max L. Gaver
James W. Golladay, Jr.
E. Donald Hardin
C. Lydon Harrell, Jr.

Michael Lackovitch
Dr. M. L. Lacy, II
LaVon P. Linn
James T. Luttrell, Jr.
LTC Walter M. McCracken
John P. McIntyre
Darris A. Maine
Bernard L. Odend'hal, Jr.
Hugh G. Parker, Jr.
Stewart M. L. Pollard
Col. J. O. Renalds
Allen E. Roberts
Dr. Orlando F. Salinas
Cecil C. Smart, Jr.
Springfield Lodge No. 217
Foy K. Vaughan, Jr.
John C. Williams

WASHINGTON
Don L. Arnold
George R. Bordewick
Stanley E. Brautigam
Gilbert L. Duffy
Charles M. Johnston
Alden H. Jones
Dr. Marlowe H. Jones
John M. Moe
Vernon R. Parks
Melvin L. Pfankuche
Fred H. Pounder
J. Stanley Ray
Donald R. Schroder
Earl B. Thomas
Robert W. Young

WEST VIRGINIA
Albert Klele, Jr.
Taft Rice
Charles Thornburg

WISCONSIN
John S. Brosemer
Irving R. Dietscher
Cecil T. Forehand
Kenneth W. Grant
Allan E. Iding
Bernard Killoran
Dr. Jules D. Levin
Dale R. Machalleck
Lester C. Noerr
Robert V. Osborne
James S. Panos
George R. Rankin
Charles L. Roblee
Donald M. Ross
Charles E. White

WYOMING
Robert W. LeGoff
Harold L. Mai

CANADA

NEW BRUNSWICK
I. Dale Steeves

NOVA SCOTIA
Wallace Smith

ONTARIO
J. S. Basarke
Dr. John R. Brown
William G. Bunker
Peter Corbin
W. J. Curtis
Bruce A. Findlay
Alan Davis Hogg
Brendan W. Larrabee
Balfour LeGresley
Wallace E. McLeod
John E. Reichert
Clifford E. Rich
Lorne K. Shrum
Gordon H. Stuart
Brien B. Thurston

QUEBEC
Robert A. Gordon

SASKATCHEWAN
Kenneth L. Melsted

FOREIGN COUNTRIES

AUSTRALIA
John J. Eddy

BAHAMAS
Ernest S. Larkin

CANAL ZONE
Engelbert J. Berger

DENMARK
Poul Malmgren

ENGLAND
Cyril N. Batham
Harry Carr
A. W. Jary
Gerald Mail
S. L. Mullins
Frederick Smyth
Howard A. Stokes

FRANCE
Jean Baylot

GERMANY
Rainer J. Schicke

HOLLAND
Order of Freemasons under the
    Grand East, Netherlands

IRAN
Dr. Ali Moarefi

ISRAEL
Reuven Trostler

ITALY
Bruno Guglielmi

MALAYSIA
The Read Temple Committee

NEW ZEALAND
Rotorua Masonic Library

WEST AFRICA
Andre A. G. Bassou

WEST INDIES
James H. Johnson
Lionel A. Seemungal

Colophon

D'ASSIGNY

Eight hundred eighty-eight copies of this limited edition were typeset, printed and bound by Pantagraph Printing Company of Bloomington, Illinois.

The type faces used in this book are of the Linotype Janson and the Montoype Garamond families. A number of facsimile pages, decorations and initial letters reproduced in this volume were photographed directly from previous editions of the books. Certain portions of the copy were typewriter-prepared by the publisher.

The text paper used is eighty pound basis softwhite Mohawk Superfine Text, smooth finish, manufactured by Mohawk Paper Mills, Inc. The book covers are made of Columbia Mills' Riverside Vellum over board and stamped in gold.

All volumes of The Masonic Book Club series were designed and prepared by Louis L. Williams, Alphonse Cerza and Fred A. Dolan.

[This text appeared in the original.]

Related Titles from Westphalia Press

Ancient Mysteries and Modern Masonry: The Collected Writings of Jewel P. Lightfoot, Edited by Billy J. Hamilton Jr.

Jewel P. Lightfoot. Former Attorney General of the State of Texas. Past Grand Master of the Masonic Grand Lodge of Texas. From humble beginnings in rural Arkansas, he worked to become an educated man who excelled in law and Freemasonry. He was a gentleman of his time, well-known as a scholar, public speaker, and Masonic philosopher.

Essay on The Mysteries and the True Object of The Brotherhood of Freemasons
by Jason Williams

This isn't a reprint of a classic. It's a new rendition with new life breathed into it, to be enjoyed both by the layperson trying to understand the Craft and Masonic scholars taking a deeper dive into the fraternity's golden years—when the concepts of liberty and equality were still fresh.

Female Emancipation and Masonic Membership: An Essential Collection
By Guillermo De Los Reyes Heredia

Female Emancipation and Masonic Membership: An Essential Combination is a collection of essays on Freemasonry and gender that promotes a transatlantic discussion of the study of the history of women and Freemasonry and their contribution in different countries.

Freemasonry, Heir to the Enlightenment
by Cécile Révauger

Modern Freemasonry may have mythical roots in Solomon's time but is really the heir to the Enlightenment. Ever since the early eighteenth century freemasons have endeavored to convey the values of the Enlightenment in the cultural, political and religious fields, in Europe, the American colonies and the emerging United States.

Freemasonry: A French View
by Roger Dachez and Alain Bauer

Perhaps one should speak not of Freemasonry but of Freemasonries in the plural. In each country Masonic historiography has developed uniqueness. Two of the best known French Masonic scholars present their own view of the worldwide evolution and challenging mysteries of the fraternity over the centuries.

Worlds of Print: The Moral Imagination of an Informed Citizenry, 1734 to 1839
by John Slifko

John Slifko argues that freemasonry was representative and played an important role in a larger cultural transformation of literacy and helped articulate the moral imagination of an informed democratic citizenry via fast emerging worlds of print.

Why Thirty-Three?: Searching for Masonic Origins
by S. Brent Morris, PhD

What "high degrees" were in the United States before 1830? What were the activities of the Order of the Royal Secret, the precursor of the Scottish Rite? A complex organization with a lengthy pedigree like Freemasonry has many basic foundational questions waiting to be answered, and that's what this book does: answers questions.

The Great Transformation: Scottish Freemasonry 1725-1810
by Dr. Mark C. Wallace

This book examines Scottish Freemasonry in its wider British and European contexts between the years 1725 and 1810. The Enlightenment effectively crafted the modern mason and propelled Freemasonry into a new era marked by growing membership and the creation of the Grand Lodge of Scotland.

Getting the Third Degree: Fraternalism, Freemasonry and History
Edited by Guillermo De Los Reyes and Paul Rich

As this engaging collection demonstrates, the doors being opened on the subject range from art history to political science to anthropology, as well as gender studies, sociology and more. The organizations discussed may insist on secrecy, but the research into them belies that.

A Place in the Lodge: Dr. Rob Morris, Freemasonry and the Order of the Eastern Star
by Nancy Stearns Theiss, PhD

Ridiculed as "petticoat masonry," critics of the Order of the Eastern Star did not deter Rob Morris' goal to establish a Masonic organization that included women as members. Morris carried the ideals of Freemasonry through a despairing time of American history.

Brought to Light: The Mysterious George Washington Masonic Cave
by Jason Williams MD

The George Washington Masonic Cave near Charles Town, West Virginia, contains a signature carving of George Washington dated 1748. This book painstakingly pieces together the chronicled events and real estate archives related to the cavern in order to sort out fact from fiction.

Dudley Wright: Writer, Truthseeker & Freemason
by John Belton

Dudley Wright (1868-1950) was an Englishman and professional journalist who took a universalist approach to the various great Truths of Life. He travelled though many religions in his life and wrote about them all, but was probably most at home with Islam.

History of the Grand Orient of Italy
Emanuela Locci, Editor

No book in Masonic literature upon the history of Italian Freemasonry has been edited in English up to now. This work consists of eight studies, covering a span from the Eighteenth Century to the end of the WWII, tracing through the story, the events and pursuits related to the Grand Orient of Italy.

westphaliapress.org

Policy Studies Organization

The Policy Studies Organization (PSO) is a publisher of academic journals and book series, sponsor of conferences, and producer of programs.

Policy Studies Organization publishes dozens of journals on a range of topics, such as European Policy Analysis, Journal of Elder Studies, Indian Politics & Polity, Journal of Critical Infrastructure Policy, and Popular Culture Review.

Additionally, Policy Studies Organization hosts numerous conferences. These conferences include the Middle East Dialogue, Space Education and Strategic Applications Conference, International Criminology Conference, Dupont Summit on Science, Technology and Environmental Policy, World Conference on Fraternalism, Freemasonry and History, and the Internet Policy & Politics Conference.

For more information on these projects, access videos of past events, and upcoming events, please visit us at:

www.ipsonet.org

www.ingramcontent.com/pod-product-compliance
Lightning Source LLC
Chambersburg PA
CBHW051546020426
42333CB00016B/2116